WITHDRAWN
PALOS VERDES LIBRARY DISTRICT

COLLECT YOUR JUDGMENT IN 5 EASY STEPS

BY ADRIENNE M. MCMILLAN
ATTORNEY AT LAW

SPHINX® PUBLISHING
AN IMPRINT OF SOURCEBOOKS, INC.®
NAPERVILLE, ILLINOIS
www.SphinxLegal.com

MAY 0 5 2008
Palos Verdes Library District

Copyright © 2007 by Adrienne M. McMillan
Cover and internal design © 2007 by Sourcebooks, Inc.®
All rights reserved. No part of this book may be reproduced in any form or by any electronic or mechanical means including information storage and retrieval systems—except in the case of brief quotations embodied in critical articles or reviews—without permission in writing from its publisher, Sourcebooks, Inc. Purchasers of the book are granted license to use the forms contained herein for their own personal use. No claim of copyright is made to any government form reproduced herein. All brand names and product names used in this book are trademarks, registered trademarks, or trade names of their respective holders. Sourcebooks and the colophon are registered trademarks of Sourcebooks, Inc.

First Edition: 2007

Published by: **Sphinx® Publishing, An Imprint of Sourcebooks, Inc.®**

Naperville Office
P.O. Box 4410
Naperville, Illinois 60567-4410
630-961-3900
Fax: 630-961-2168
www.sourcebooks.com
www.SphinxLegal.com

This publication is designed to provide accurate and authoritative information in regard to the subject matter covered. It is sold with the understanding that the publisher is not engaged in rendering legal, accounting, or other professional service. If legal advice or other expert assistance is required, the services of a competent professional person should be sought.

From a Declaration of Principles Jointly Adopted by a Committee of the American Bar Association and a Committee of Publishers and Associations

This product is not a substitute for legal advice.

Disclaimer required by Texas statutes.

Library of Congress Cataloging-in-Publication Data
McMillan, Adrienne M.
  Collect your judgment in 5 easy steps / by Adrienne M. McMillan. --
1st ed.
    p. cm.
  ISBN-13: 978-1-57248-635-5 (pbk. : alk. paper)
  ISBN-10: 1-57248-635-X (pbk. : alk. paper)
  1. Collection laws--United States--Popular works. 2. Debtor and
creditor--United States--Popular works. I. Title. II. Title: Collect your judgment in five easy steps.
  KF1024.Z9M36 2007
  346.7307'7--dc22
                                                    2007025436

Printed and bound in the United States of America
SB — 10 9 8 7 6 5 4 3 2 1

Contents

Who is Your Debtor?
Your Judgment
Appeal
Due Date
Statute of Limitations
Interest
Sample Interest Chart
Renew Your Judgment
Judgment Worksheet
Correcting Your Judgment

Disclaimer

No warranties or guarantees are given to any purchaser or end user of this book. This book is only intended for informational purposes and is not to be considered legal advice. It should not be relied on in place of the advice of an attorney. It is intended to teach individuals how to collect their own judgments.

Neither the author nor the publisher of this book shall be liable for any errors in the content, nor for any actions taken in reliance thereon. Furthermore, neither the author nor the publisher shall be liable for any damages or costs of any type arising out of, or in any way connected with, the use of this book by any purchaser or end user.

It is the responsibility of the individual using this book to educate him- or herself on the laws of the state in which he or she collects his or her judgment.

There are many procedures available to help you collect your judgment. The more complicated, uncommon procedures are not recommended until you have exhausted the more common procedures discussed in this book. If you find yourself facing a particularly complicated case, you may need to do further research. This book will give you a foundation on which to build your knowledge. We recommend that you take notes on the issues that you would like to look up in your jurisdiction while working your way through the five steps.

Dedication

This book is dedicated to my parents, Pat and Ed Smith, for all of their love and support.

Introduction

Many states have recognized the trend sweeping through the courts of parties, sometimes on both sides of the case, representing themselves. Even in cases in which one or more of the parties are represented at trial, once a judgment is entered, many attorneys *substitute* out of the case and the winner is left to collect his or her own judgment.

Many courts are offering assistance by launching informational websites. However, these sites are vague and complicated, and in the end, they often suggest you enlist the services of an attorney. Maybe you were told after your hearing to consult or hire an attorney, but then you found out that an attorney will cost you up to 50% of your judgment. You might even have been told, "Go ahead and execute on your judgment," without any further instruction at all.

Every day, thousands of people resolve their disputes in court without seeking the advice of an attorney, in part due to the new self-help centers now available in courthouses across the country.

Many people teach themselves to collect their own judgments. However, just like anything else, it takes longer to teach yourself than it does to be taught by someone else. This book will give you the assistance you need. It will teach you what you need to know to get your money in just five easy-to-follow steps. You can enforce your judgment all by yourself. The process is not that difficult—all you need is a little instruction.

It is not necessary to read the entire book before you begin. It is recommended that you read through the Step 1 chapters before proceeding. Then follow each step. If you hit a stumbling block, back up and reread the preceding section.

JUDGMENT WORKSHEET

It is important to identify your debtor, your debtor's assets, your state's laws, and the court rules that apply to your judgment. Before you begin collecting your judgment, complete your worksheet with as much information as you can locate (see page 4). Start by looking on your court's website, if it has one. If you are unable to get all of the information that you need, visit your courthouse and speak to a few of the clerks.

FORMS

Many states have created standardized forms to help self-represented litigants, like you, navigate their way through the system. Many sample forms are included in Appendix C to get you used to seeing and working with them. The best way to get comfortable with these forms is just to fill them out. The information requested on each form is numbered. Start with #1 and continue through the form without skipping any numbers. If you are asked for information that you do not know, make it up. This exercise is simply to get you used to reading the forms carefully and providing the requested information.

Some standardized forms are mandatory, while others are optional. Look at the bottom of each form, usually off to one side, for the form to either say "optional" or "mandatory." You should get a copy of the forms available in your state. If your state does not provide forms, or only provides a few, practice completing forms by using the sample forms in Appendix C of this book. If forms are not available in your state, ask one of the clerks for samples (if available) of pleadings used in your court.

To look for forms in your state, do the following.

- Access your court's website or visit the clerk's office in your local court-house.
- Get two of each form they provide for judgments.
- Read through each form carefully.
- If the form refers to "plaintiff" and "defendant," put it in one pile; if the form refers to "judgment creditor" and "judgment debtor," put it in another pile. Forms used post-judgment usually refer to the parties as "judgment creditor" and "judgment debtor," so those in that pile are most likely the forms you will need to collect your judgment. The remaining forms, the ones that only use the terms "plaintiff" and "defendant," are probably pre-judgment forms that you do not need anymore.

- Make a list of the forms you have in your post-judgment pile.
- Separate your post-judgment pile into two sets.
- Put one set aside to keep for the real thing.
- Take the second set and start filling them out. Get familiar with the format. Highlight any questions that you do not understand.
- Keep your practice set to reference when you start filling out the real set. (You will find filled-in forms for a sample judgment collection in Appendix B, which you can refer to throughout the process.)

LEGAL TERMS

Each state determines which procedures are available to collect civil judgments issued by its courts. Even though the procedures used in your state may be similar to those of other states, the terms that your state uses can be a little different, and sometimes they might be very different. If you are unable to find a particular term in your jurisdiction, or the court clerk looks at you like you are speaking a different language, try explaining the procedure instead of using a specific term. The procedures are pretty much the same.

For example, you may hear the term "judgment collection" referred to as "judgment enforcement" or "judgment execution." All of these terms mean the same thing. Do not focus on the term used in your state—focus on the big picture.

STEP 1

UNDERSTAND THE PROCESS

You and Your Debtor

It is a good idea to start by getting to know all of the players involved in the judgment collection process. Remember, during your lawsuit, you were called "plaintiff" and the other party was called "defendant." Now that you have a judgment in your favor, your new title is *judgment creditor* or just *creditor.* Your defendant's new title is *judgment debtor* or just *debtor.*

It is important for you to know that not all debtors are the same. There are people who simply do not have anything for you to take; they are called *judgment proof debtors.* A judgment proof debtor could be someone who has so little property and few prospects of getting anything in the future that attempting to pursue him or her for your money would be so troublesome that it would not be worth your time. If your debtor is such a person, then no matter how many books you read, you will not be able to get your money. You are better off preserving your sanity and walking away from the whole thing. Hopefully, this information does not apply to your case.

How can you tell whether your debtor is judgment proof? It is difficult to generalize, but here are some guidelines that will start you in the right direction. If you can answer yes to any of these questions, you may have a judgment proof debtor on your hands:

- Is your debtor incarcerated and not expected to get released in the next ten years?
- Is your debtor elderly, living off Social Security, and taking the bus?
- Is your debtor being chased by the law or the IRS?
- Is your debtor behind on child support payments?
- Is your debtor leaving the country permanently?
- Is your debtor permanently disabled and living solely on disability?
- Does your debtor already have several judgments against him or her?

If you think your debtor is NOT judgment proof but he or she still has not sent you your money, ask for the money. Write a brief letter and ask him or her to pay you. You would be surprised to learn how many people will actually send a check just to get some closure. (See a sample demand letter in Appendix D.) If you do not receive any response, or the response you do receive is not satisfactory, keep reading.

WHO IS YOUR DEBTOR?

It is crucial that you understand exactly who your judgment is against before you start to collect. It sounds like a strange thing to say, but read this section on the different kinds of debtors to understand why this is an important step.

Individuals

If you sued an individual because of something that person did in his or her personal capacity, like hit your car or failed to pay you back the

$300 you loaned him or her, then his or her personal assets are subject to your judgment.

Businesses

If you sued a business, like the dry cleaner that damaged your leather jacket or the car dealer that sold you a lemon, you need to determine whether your debtor is an entity or a person, or both. If you see "DBA," which stands for "doing business as" on your judgment, then you have the business and the owner to pursue. You may also see "trading as," which means the same thing as "DBA."

For example, your dry cleaner is owned by a woman named Susan Hernandez. Your judgment reads, "Defendant, Susan Hernandez DBA Sunshine Dry Cleaners, owes Plaintiff $850.00." This means that you sued Susan Hernandez personally and in her business capacity as "Sunshine Dry Cleaners." You can go after Susan Hernandez's personal assets, like her car and house, and the business assets of Sunshine Dry Cleaners, like the cash register or checking account.

In another instance, if you sued the car dealer and your judgment reads "Defendant, New City Cars, Inc., owes Plaintiff $5,000," or "Defendant, New City Cars, LLC, owes Plaintiff $5,000," then you can only enforce your judgment against the assets of the entity. The abbreviation "Inc." stands for "incorporated." The abbreviation "LLC" stands for "limited liability company," which operates just like a corporation. Both of these types of businesses are entities and not people, so there is not one owner to pursue. In corporations there are *shareholders,* and in limited liability companies there are *members.* Both members and shareholders are protected from any liability resulting from their businesses' operations.

YOUR JUDGMENT

Once you are able to identify your debtor, you must understand a few facts about your judgment before you can proceed with collecting your judgment. Every case has an identifying number, called a *case number,* sometimes called a *suit number* or a *docket number.* You were assigned that number when you filed your case and you have continued to write that number on your paperwork, along with the names of the parties. Make sure you always continue to reference your case number on all of the paperwork you file while collecting your judgment. That information, in addition to the names of the parties, is called the *case caption.*

APPEAL

Most states give one or both parties the right to appeal the decision of the court. If you are in a state that allows at least one party to appeal, you will have to wait for that time to pass. The court issues a *stay of enforcement* during that time period, and this prevents you from beginning to collect your judgment. The average time for filing an appeal from a judgment is thirty days.

If no appeal is filed before the expiration of the appeal period, you can begin to collect your money.

In some states, the party filing an appeal is required to file a bond with the court. If this is required in your state, contact the clerk's office that handles appeals to find out how to get that bond money if the appeal is denied. You will probably have to file a motion, *ex parte* (meaning that all parties do not have to be present), asking the court for an order directing your court's accounting department to release the money to you.

DUE DATE

Some states take a more proactive approach to assisting creditors, like you, in collecting their judgments.

Michigan and Kentucky, for example, set a *due date* by when your debtor must have paid your judgment. If your debtor failed to pay you by that date, you would file for a court order directing your debtor to appear in court to answer why he or she has not paid you. In Michigan, if your debtor does not pay you within twenty-one days of the entry of your judgment, he or she must send you a completed *affidavit of judgment debtor.*

If your state does not have a due date, then all you need to do is wait out the time for an appeal. Once the appeal period expires, you can start collecting your money.

STATUTE OF LIMITATIONS

Most judgments are *good* for a period of years, determined by each state, and this period is called a *statute of limitations.* In most cases, you will have plenty of time to collect your money. There are a few states that have fairly short statutes of limitations, so verify by checking with your state laws to make sure you have time remaining.

In California, if your judgment is for *family support* (e.g., child support), it does not have a statute of limitations. You can continue to collect your judgment without the need to renew it. If your judgment is for family support, check your state's code of civil procedure, or its equivalent, to determine if a statute of limitations applies.

If you have had your judgment for several years, you need to make sure it is not about to expire. If you fail to renew your judgment before it expires, you will lose it forever. There are very few exceptions to a statute of limitations. Check your state's code of civil procedure, or its equivalent, to determine if such an exception exists in your case.

If you are approaching that time, you need to renew your judgment before proceeding. (See "Renew your Judgment" on page 10.)

INTEREST

All judgments earn interest every year in an amount determined by each state. Look up your state's interest rate and write that information on your judgment worksheet (see page 11).

Now you know how long you have to collect your judgment and how much interest you will be earning each year.

The interest you are earning on your judgment is probably *simple interest,* not compound interest. Simple interest does not get added to the principal amount of your judgment. All the interest that you earn stays in the interest category until you renew your judgment. At that time, you add the interest and *post-judgment costs* (costs added after your judgment was entered) to the *principal* (the amount the court awarded you, not including costs). You then start earning interest on your new principal amount. The chart on page 9 is an example of a judgment that was renewed after the eighth year and is in a state that allows 10% simple interest.

Sample Interest Chart

Entered 1/1/94	Judgment	Principal	Interest	Cost
Year 1 (1994)	$5022.00	$5000.00	$0	$22.00
Year 2 (1995)	$5022.00	$5000.00	$500.00	$22.00
Year 3 (1996)	$5022.00	$5000.00	$1000.00	$22.00
Year 4 (1997)	$5022.00	$5000.00	$1500.00	$22.00
Year 5 (1998)	$5022.00	$5000.00	$2000.00	$22.00
Year 6 (1999)	$5022.00	$5000.00	$2500.00	$22.00
Year 7 (2000)	$5022.00	$5000.00	$3000.00	$22.00
Year 8 (2001)	$5022.00	$5000.00	$3500.00	$22.00
Renew	**$8522.00**	**$8500.00**	**$0**	**$22.00**
Year 1 (2002)	$8522.00	$8500.00	$850.00	$22.00
Year 2 (2003)	$8522.00	$8500.00	$1700.00	$22.00
Year 3 (2004)	$8522.00	$8500.00	$2550.00	$22.00
Year 4 (2005)	$8522.00	$8500.00	$3400.00	$22.00
Year 5 (2006)	$8522.00	$8500.00	$4250.00	$22.00
Year 6 (2007)	$8522.00	$8500.00	$5100.00	$22.00
Year 7 (2008)	$8522.00	$8500.00	$5950.00	$22.00

After the eighth year, you are earning 10% interest on $8,500—not too bad. You might wonder why you wouldn't just renew your judgment every year so you can keep adding your interest to the principal amount. The answer is that most states only allow you to renew your judgment once every five years after the first time you renew it.

In California, you can renew your judgment at any time the first time you renew it. You can only renew it every five years after the first renewal.

RENEW YOUR JUDGMENT

If your judgment is about to expire, you should renew it before beginning collections. Remember, all of the interest you have earned from the date your judgment was entered to the date you renew your judgment should be added to the principal of your judgment. After your judgment is renewed, the new amount should reflect your original judgment amount, prejudgment costs (added by the court), post-judgment costs, and interest earned, minus any payments received.

To renew your judgment, do the following.

- Get the forms required in your state to renew your judgment. You will probably need several forms. (In California, for example, you need a Notice of Renewal of Judgment, an Application for Renewal of Judgment, and a Memorandum of Costs.)
- Complete the forms.
- Make at least three copies of each form.
- File the forms with the clerk of the court that entered your judgment.
- Mail your debtor a copy of each form.
- Return a proof of service to the court.

Now you will write down what you have learned about your judgment and your debtor on your Judgment Worksheet. Your goal here is to recall as much information as you can about your debtor and his or her finances. Move on to page 11 and fill in as much information as you have. Do not worry if you do not know some of the information requested. You will continue to fill in the information throughout the entire collection process.

Judgment Worksheet

Your Judgment

Case number _____

Date entered _____

Principal amount _____ Costs (prejudgment) _____

Interest _____

Appeal period starts _____ Ends _____

Statute of limitations _____ Interest rate _____

Information about the Court that Entered Your Judgment

Phone number (answered by a human, not machine)

_____

Court self-help website

_____

In-person help:

Location _____

Hours _____ Phone _____

Email _____

Personal Information about Your Debtor (Person or Business)

Debtor's name _____

Age/Years in Operation _____ Profession/Industry _____

Marital status _____

If married, partnered, or otherwise legally bound, list name of that other

person _____

Children _____ If yes, provide names and ages

_____

_____

Debtor's Social Security number _____
DOB _____
Driver's license number and state _____
Current address _____
City _____ State _____ Zip _____
Phone (h) _____ (w) _____
Physical description: Ht. _____ Wt. _____
Eye color _____ Hair color _____

Debtor's Bank Accounts

Checking account _____ Branch _____
Checking account _____ Branch _____
Checking account _____ Branch _____
Savings account _____ Branch _____
Savings account _____ Branch _____
Savings account _____ Branch _____

Debtor's Automobiles

Make _____ Model _____
Year _____ Color _____
Make _____ Model _____
Year _____ Color _____
Make _____ Model _____
Year _____ Color _____

Debtor's Employment (Individual Debtor)

Current Employer

_____

_____

Address _____

City _____ State _____ Zip _____

Salary _____

Previous Employer

_____

_____

Address _____

City _____ State _____ Zip _____

Salary _____

Rental Properties Debtor Owns

Address _____

City _____ State_____ Zip _____

Address _____

City _____ State _____ Zip _____

Address _____

City _____ State _____ Zip _____

Jewelry Debtor Owns

Describe piece_____ Est. value _____

Describe piece_____ Est. value _____

Describe piece_____ Est. value _____

Describe piece_____ Est. value _____

Debtor's Other Income Sources

Source _____

Amount _____ Monthly/Weekly/Daily

Source _____

Amount _____ Monthly/Weekly/Daily

Any information not mentioned: _____

_____

_____

_____

_____

_____

_____

_____

_____

_____

CORRECTING YOUR JUDGMENT

If your debtor's name is misspelled on your judgment, you have to have it corrected before you can start collecting your judgment. For example, your judgment debtor is listed on your judgment as "Johnny" instead of "John." Check with the clerk's office to see if your court has a standardized form for this procedure. If there is not a standardized form, you will have to draft a motion. If you do have to draft your request, call it "Judgment Creditor's Motion to Correct Judgment Debtor's Name on Judgment."

If you figure out that you actually sued the wrong person or only sued the business name and not the owner (if it is a sole proprietorship or partnership), you cannot use this method to add a new debtor. Out of fear of people adding a new party to a judgment that never had notice of a lawsuit, courts are cautious when correcting judgments. You should provide as much information as it takes to prove that your request to correct your judgment is not adding a new party.

It is hoped that you did some research into exactly how to name your defendant before you filed your lawsuit. Once your judgment is entered, the name on your judgment is the name of the person or business you will be collecting from. If there is a mistake, whether it is your mistake or the court's mistake, you have to get a court order to correct it.

ENFORCEMENT COSTS

All reasonable costs that you incur while attempting to collect your judgment should be added to your judgment. You need to keep accurate records and receipts for all the money that you spend while collecting your judgment. Check your state's procedural laws to determine which expenses are allowable. Usually, you have to add your expenses to your judgment within a specific time period. In California, you must add your expenses within two years from when they are incurred.

A Memorandum of Costs or something similarly named is what you need to add post-judgment costs and interest to your judgment. You should get into the habit of completing one every few months to ensure that the interest your judgment has earned is recognized by the court. If your state does not use a standardized form, then consult a practice guide or a forms guide in your local law library for direction in drafting your own. Any procedure that you initiate in an effort to collect your money will probably cost you money, so you need to keep track of your expenses and add them to your judgment.

CREDITING PAYMENTS RECEIVED

It is very important that you keep accurate records of your judgment's balance, costs added, and interest earned. The *Sample Interest Chart* on page 9 demonstrated how to keep track of your interest until your judgment is renewed. The *Sample Monthly Chart* on page 17 demonstrates not only how to keep track of your costs, but how to credit payments received. To keep track of your numbers, you should create a chart similar to the one on page 17. Include the following six categories in your chart:

1. Judgment Principle
2. Prejudgment Costs
3. Prejudgment Interest
4. Post-judgment Costs Added
5. Post-judgment Interest Added
6. Payments Received and Credited

Your chart can be weekly, monthly, or yearly. It depends on how often you expect to enter new costs, interests, and credit payments.

If you receive a payment that is larger than the total amount that you have earned in interest, credit the total amount you have earned in interest and then credit the remainder to the principal section.

Sample Monthly Chart

Your $5,000 judgment accrues 10% simple interest annually. You receive a payment of $200 from your debtor, so you need your chart to reflect that credit.

Judgment	Pre-J Costs	Pre-J Interest	Post-J Costs	Post-J Interest	Payments
5000.00	22.00	0	0	0	0
5000.00	22.00	0	44.00	+41.66	
5000.00 −116.68 = 4883.32	22.00	0	100.00 + 44.00 = 144.00	41.66 +41.66 = 83.32–83.32 = 0	200.00

In this chart, each new line represents a new month. The first line is the first month you received your judgment, so it represents the principal amount of your judgment, costs, and no pre-judgment interest, no post-judgment costs, and no interest. The second line, representing the second month, shows you spent $44.00 in costs trying to collect your judgment. The interest you have earned is $41.66.

The third line, representing the third month, shows you spent $100.00 in costs trying to collect your judgment, which brings your total post-judgment costs to $144.00. You earned another $41.66 in interest, bringing the total interest earned to $83.32. You then received a payment of $200.00. Enter the $200.00 payment into the "Payments" column and start to deduct the amount from the "Post-J Interest" column. Since you have only earned $83.32 of interest, you only credit (subtract) $83.32 of the payment from the interest column, leaving $116.68 from the $200.00 payment. Next, credit (subtract) that $116.68 to the $5,000.00 principal, leaving a balance of $4,883.32.

It is up to you to keep track of your costs, interest, and payments received. If you are not careful, you may end up shorting yourself. Be careful!

To add interest and costs to your judgment, do the following.

- Get your state's standardized form (if available), probably called a Memorandum of Costs.
- Complete the form.
- If you are only adding interest, file the form with the clerk in the courthouse that entered your judgment.
- If you are adding costs and interest, have someone *serve* (deliver) a copy to your debtor and complete a proof of service.
- File the form and the completed proof of service with the clerk in the courthouse that entered your judgment.

Note: If your court does not have a standardized form, draft your own and continue with the next step. (See a sample, not a standardized, Memorandum of Costs in Appendix C.)

Any time you are filing a Memorandum of Costs, *always* calculate and add your earned interest.

You should periodically add your costs to your judgment by completing and filing a Memorandum of Costs. You do not want to hold on to all of your receipts and try to add the costs on at the end. Remember, you can usually only add costs within a certain time period. Also, if your debtor pays off your judgment directly to the court, those costs that you have not added are history. Keep up on it.

The Legal System

The legal system can be scary and overwhelming, probably because most people who encounter the legal system do so involuntarily. Keep in mind that you do not have to learn every law ever written to collect your judgment. You only have to familiarize yourself with the procedural laws for your court, the rules that govern courts in your state, and the local rules that govern how things in your particular courthouse work.

CIVIL PROCEDURE LAWS

Civil procedure is the body of law that dictates how things will progress in civil proceedings, as opposed to criminal proceedings. Your lawsuit was governed by your state's law of civil procedure. Some states do not break down their laws into different codes and name one of them "civil procedure." Your state may only have one code that includes all laws made through your *state legislature* (state government). For purposes of collecting your judgment, you will only have to be concerned with those codes that pertain to civil procedure, so be sure to find those applicable laws for your state. You need not concern yourself with criminal laws.

COURT RULES AND LOCAL RULES OF COURT

Court rules are created to ensure uniformity in court procedures throughout your state. Local rules are created to ensure uniformity within your courthouse. These rules prevent people from *forum shopping*—choosing one court over another in an attempt to get a better outcome. You will have to check both the state court rules and your local rules if you have questions pertaining to how documents are filed, how many copies to bring, and so on. Just familiarize yourself with the table of contents so you at least know where to look for something when you have a question. You will also need to understand when something is mandatory and when something is optional. Keep in mind the following language:

"Shall" and "must" = mandatory (you have to)
"May" = permissive (you can, but do not have to)
"Should" = indicates a strong suggestion (you do not have to, but probably should)
"Will" = indicates a future happening or predicts action by a court but does not say you have to now

CODES VS. CASE LAW

Laws that are *codified*—written and numbered into sections called *codes*—are laws created by your state legislature. Courts interpret your state's codes in lawsuits, and the court's findings in those cases are called *case law.* For example, if your state legislature made it illegal to punch another person, it might write a law and put it in the *state penal code* (criminal laws) in this manner:

Battery: The intentional infliction of a harmful or offensive touching of another is a felony.

The lawyers in the case would argue different interpretations of "touching." The court would have to choose which interpretation of the word is correct. That court's finding is called case law and is binding on lower courts in your state. You will most likely not have to research case law to collect your judgment, but this explanation is provided just in case it comes up.

FEDERAL COLLECTION LAWS

The following section covers the federal laws that pertain to judgment collection. You should understand the importance of these laws and be able to locate them should you need to do further research.

Fair Debt Collection Practices Act

The *Fair Debt Collection Practices Act* (FDCPA) prohibits abusive, deceptive, and otherwise improper collection practices by third-party collectors. The FDCPA describes a *debt* as any obligation or alleged obligation of a consumer to pay money arising out of a transaction in which the money, property, insurance, or service that is the subject of the transaction is primarily for personal, family, or household purposes, whether or not such obligation has been reduced to a judgment. This law applies only to debt collectors—not you.

A *debt collector* is described as any person who uses any business, the principal purpose of which is the collection of any debts, or who regularly collects or attempts to collect, directly or indirectly, debts owed or due or asserted to be owed or due to another. An individual collecting his or her own debt is NOT a debt collector, so the FDCPA does not apply to you. However, just because this law does not apply to you does not mean you should engage in any of the conduct it prohibits. The main purpose of the FDCPA is to prohibit harassment of a debtor, so you should keep this in mind as you collect your judgment.

For more in-depth coverage, refer to 15 U.S.C. 1601 et seq. (Volume 15 of the United States Code, Section 1601 and the following.)

The Fair Credit Reporting Act

The *Fair Credit Reporting Act* (FCRA) governs the information that companies can supply concerning consumer credit. The FCRA allows only businesses with legitimate business needs to obtain credit reports. This is the law that prohibits you from obtaining your debtor's credit report. If you are only collecting your own judgment, then you are NOT in the business of collecting judgments. Therefore, you would not have a legitimate business need and would not be permitted to obtain credit reports. For more in-depth coverage, refer to 15 U.S.C. 1681 et seq. You can access the complete text of this act at **www.ftc.gov**.

The Gramm-Leach-Bliley Act

The *Gramm-Leach-Bliley Act* concerns the privacy of individuals' bank or financial records. A common practice in judgment collection is called *pretexting*, in which you call a bank and pretend to be a merchant who is trying to find out if a check you have been given by your debtor will clear. If your debtor wrote you a check for any reason or you wrote your debtor

a check (and if he or she deposited that check into his or her ban]
you would have his or her account number on the back) you ·
his or her bank and see if his or her account is still open and currently nas
enough money to pay your judgment. If you found out the account was
open and had enough money, you would then initiate a bank levy. The
Gramm-Leach-Bliley Act makes pretexting a federal crime, so keep in
mind that you must never misrepresent yourself. For more in-depth
coverage, refer to 15 U.S.C. 6801 et seq.

Your state will probably also have laws that govern judgment collections.
State law usually gives the consumer greater protection than federal law.
You should also familiarize yourself with your state's collection laws. Ask
your local law librarian to lead you to your state's laws on debt collection,
or you could look in your state's civil code or its equivalent. Do not rush
out and try to memorize your state's collection laws. Just be mindful of
where to find them should you ever need to do additional research.

SERVICE OF PROCESS

A basic legal requirement common to almost all legal procedures is serving
your paperwork to the other party. *Service of process* is the act of having
someone other than yourself deliver your paperwork to the other party in
the legal procedure. There are several ways to have your paperwork served.
The most common methods of service include personal service, substitute
service, mail service, and publication. You might remember having to serve
your debtor papers during your lawsuit. You may have hired someone,
maybe even the court, to serve your debtor.

In collecting your judgment, you will probably have to serve your debtor with papers again. The most important thing to know about service of process, whether it is before judgment or after, is this: in most instances, you cannot serve your own papers.

Method of Service

Which method of service you are required to use will depend on the procedure you are implementing. When in doubt, use personal service. If you have a judgment against a corporation, limited liability company (LLC), limited liability partnership (LLP), or limited partnership (LP), then serving the agent for service is considered personal service. An *agent for service* is either an individual or a company that has been designated by the corporation, LLC, LLP, or LP to receive legal paperwork. To determine who an agent for service is, check with the secretary of state in your state, or your state's equivalent.

Personal Service

Personal service is the act of delivering your paperwork to your debtor—not mailing it or handing it to a friend, family member, or boss. It is usually considered complete the day your debtor is handed your papers. When in doubt as to what method of service to use, always use personal service.

Substitute Service

Substitute service is the act of serving someone instead of your debtor, substituting someone else in for your debtor (or with a corporation, LLC, LLP, or LP, the agent for service). Substitute service usually requires a second step. Once your server hands the paperwork to an adult resident of your debtor's home or to someone apparently in charge of his or her workplace, your server then has to mail a second copy back to the address where he or she just served the paperwork. This method of service is not available for every procedure, so check the local rules or your state's code of civil procedure to determine if you may use this method. Substitute service is usually considered complete a certain number of days after the second copy has been put into the mail. For example, in California, substitute service is considered complete ten days from the mailing date.

Service by Mail

Serving your papers through the mail is just what it sounds like. You have someone other than yourself who is not a party to your case (not a co-creditor on your judgment) put your papers in the mail and complete a proof of service for you. Remember that you must always file your completed proof of service with the court.

Proof of Service

Regardless of which method of service you use, the person serving your papers—your server—must be someone who is not a party to your case. Some states have specific requirements about who the server must be. For example, in Minnesota, your paperwork must be served by a sheriff's deputy, process server, or someone over age 18 who does not have any financial interest in your case.

Your server must also complete a *proof of service* form (also called a *certificate of service*) after your paperwork has been served. You then have to return your proof of service or certificate of service to the court immediately. (See Appendix C for a sample proof of service.)

Process Servers and the Sheriff's Department

It is strongly recommended that you hire the civil division of the sheriff's department (also called constable or marshall) or a *process server* to deliver your papers. It can be a pain in the neck to serve someone, so save your friends and family members the headache and hire someone else to do it. It is not usually that expensive and you can add the cost to your judgment by filing a Memorandum of Costs.

If you decide to go with a process server, call around to different companies to get quotes before you hire anyone. You will have to pay extra if you want your debtor served before or after business hours, or on the weekend. Also, it will probably cost a good deal more if you need someone to stake out your debtor's place to serve him or her.

The sheriff's department will not usually serve after hours and will not stake out your debtor's place. If you need to serve your debtor after hours or on the weekend, or if you need his or her place staked out, hire a process server. The best place to find a process server is in the Yellow Pages.

If time is not an issue, use the sheriff's department. The sheriff will not cost as much as a process server, but you also will not have as much control over when the papers are served. Determine what your needs are and go with the server that best suits you.

Levying Officer

The civil division of the sheriff's department will most likely also play a very important role later on in the collection process, as the levying officer. A *levying officer* implements most of the collection procedures that you will use to collect your judgment. Call your local sheriff's office to verify who the levying officer is in your county.

REFERENCE MATERIALS

At some point while collecting your judgment, you may need to draft a motion, write a declaration, or cite a code section. To do so, you will need to do a little research into your own state's procedural laws. Before you run into a situation like that, it is a good idea to become familiar with the resources that are out there and available to you for free.

Law Library

This book makes reference to your local law library. A *law library* is a library dedicated to the topic of law. You can find books on state laws, federal laws, and international laws in almost every law library. Look in the White Pages of your phone book for a law school in your area. Most law schools will allow you to use their facilities for a small admissions fee. Also, look to see if your local government has a public law library that you can use free of charge. Once you find a law library near your home, ask the law librarian for a tour. You will be surprised how much assistance you can get if you just ask.

Internet

The Internet literally has thousands of websites dedicated to the law. You can look up legal terms, download forms, and participate in chat rooms. Start your research by finding your court's website; look to see if it offers special assistance to *self-represented litigants* (that's you). It may even have forms that you can fill out online, so you will not have to make an extra trip to the courthouse to pick them up or buy them from a legal form company online. You may even be able to file your forms with the court online.

Practice Guides

If you want to see a sample of a motion or find legal-sounding language to use in a declaration that you have to write, go to your local law library and consult a practice guide. *Practice guides* are used by attorneys learning to practice in a new field of law or dabbling into areas outside of their area of expertise. You will find practice guides extremely helpful. Ask your law librarian to direct you to the practice guides in judgment collection or debt collection.

Sheriff Association's Civil Procedure Manual

Ask your local law librarian if he or she has a copy of your *sheriff association's civil procedure manual,* or anything similar to it. You can also call your local sheriff's office to see if they have a copy on hand for you to look at or purchase. This type of manual will show you step-by-step how the levying officers (usually the civil division of the sheriff's office) will implement the collection procedures you will be using (like a keeper levy or bank levy). This information can be very helpful in understanding the big picture. You can also learn a great deal of what you need to know to collect your judgment at your local courthouse.

THE COURTHOUSE

Your courthouse can be an amazing source of information when you are trying to collect your judgment. The court staff understands and can explain to you exactly how the collection procedures actually work at your courthouse.

Most of the court files are open to the public, with the exception of dependency cases, juvenile cases, adoptions, and records sealed by the court. You are free to look through the files to find out if your debtor has ever been involved in any other lawsuits. Next time you are going to your courthouse, take a few minutes to walk around and see what is available.

Special Departments

Some courts have special departments created to assist litigants in judgment collection. For example, the courts in Pennsylvania have a department called the Judgment and Petition Unit. It helps self-represented litigants through the filing of all post-judgment petitions and motions. New Jersey also has a department to help you collect your judgment called the Special Civil Part Court Officer.

Check with the court in your state to see if there is a special department or a self-help center to give you some direction.

Court Files

Court files are public records and are available for you to look through. If you find a case where your debtor lost a lawsuit and paid the creditor (the winner), contact that creditor and ask for any information on your debtor that you do not already have. Every judgment that is entered, except those sealed by the court, will be accessible to you. All you need to locate a case file is the case number, which you can look up by your debtor's name.

If your debtor has been divorced or is currently going through a divorce, you may be able to access some financial information from the case file. It is a good idea to do a general search on your debtor the next time you are at the courthouse. When collecting a judgment, you can never have too much information.

If your court has its files in a database, spend a few minutes familiarizing yourself with the program. Some databases are more user-friendly than others. Ideally, such a database would allow you to search and select files by the parties' names or the date the judgment was entered. If your courthouse does not have its files in a database, ask for assistance from the clerk in the filing room.

Court Clerks and Judicial Officers

The *court clerks* in almost every courthouse are truly the ones who actually make the courthouses function. For this reason, if you are disrespectful, you will have a very difficult time getting anything done. This cannot be emphasized enough.

When you visit the courthouse, be friendly and courteous, because there are many gray areas in the law, and these gray areas can provide you with some wiggle room. The clerks can allow you to do certain things that can make your life a lot easier, like filing a proof of service on the day of the hearing instead of several days in advance. For this reason, always be nice to the clerks.

Judicial officers are experienced attorneys who have worked very hard to get to where they are—on the bench. Treat them with respect. Refer to them as "Your Honor" when they are on the bench and "Judge _____" when off the bench. Never raise your voice at a judicial officer, and whatever you do, never tell the judicial officer that he or she is wrong. You may disagree, but once a decision has been made, it is unlikely you will change the judicial officer's mind by arguing with him or her afterwards. The bottom line is: always treat court staff with respect.

NOTE: Now that you are acquainted with your debtor, your judgment, and the legal system, read the sample cases in Appendix A to get an idea of the big picture. Then carry on with Step 2 of the collection process.

STEP 2

FIND THE MONEY

3

Where's the Money?

Now it is time to find your money. Money can come in many different forms, called assets. An *asset* is anything that is owned by or owed to your debtor that has monetary value. It can be cash, a paycheck, stocks, an interest in personal or real property, and so on.

In this section, each of the resources available to help you locate your debtor's assets is explained, and the debtor examination process is clarified, in case you have no clue whether or not your debtor even has any assets.

CREDIT REPORTS

You will probably have a friend tell you to just get a copy of your debtor's credit report, but this is unwise advice. Not everyone is allowed to get credit reports. In fact, it is difficult to qualify to get someone else's credit report. Believe it or not, having a civil judgment against someone does not usually qualify you. It is not recommended that you attempt to get your debtor's credit report.

However, if you already had a copy of your debtor's credit report before you got your judgment, you can use it to help you collect your judgment. If you extended your debtor credit or rented him or her an apartment, you may have been allowed access to his or her credit report to see if he or she was creditworthy. If so, read over it carefully to determine if there is anything in the report that you can use.

FINDING YOUR DEBTOR

Before you can start to collect your judgment, you must be able to locate your debtor. If you know where your debtor is located, skip this section and proceed to Chapter 4. If you do not know where to find your debtor, read this section carefully.

There are many ways to locate a missing debtor. It is recommended that you exhaust all sources of public information before turning to a professional, such as a private investigator or a judgment collector, to help you find your debtor.

Public Records

Government agencies keep records of people and their affairs. Many of these records are available to you to view or copy. All you have to do is go down to the government agency (you will have to pay a small fee to get copies). You may even be able to access the documents on the agency's website. The following government agencies will be the most helpful to you when trying to locate your debtor and your debtor's assets.

Recorder-Assessor's Office

A *recorder-assessor's office* typically has two functions: 1) recording documents concerning real property, like deeds when real property is sold; and, 2) determining the value of real property within the county. To find out if your debtor owns any real property, go to the recorder-assessor's office, or the county's equivalent. If you think he or she may own property in several counties, go to the recorder-assessor's office in each county. You can usually access the information by supplying your debtor's first and last name. If you suspect your debtor owns a specific piece of real property, you will need to be able to provide the clerk with the address of the piece of property in question.

County Clerk's Office

A *county clerk's office* typically keeps vital records of the people who live or conduct business in your county. You should visit the clerk's office and ask what types of records your county clerk keeps. Many county clerks now have user-friendly websites that can be used to access the clerk's records. Try the Internet first. If you do not have access to the Internet or just prefer not to, head down for an in-person visit.

The following is a partial list of the records you can usually find in a county clerk's office:

- business records (license to operate a business, fictitious business name, etc.);
- medical licenses;
- notary public records;
- assumed names;
- domestic partnership registrations; and,
- marriage records.

Fictitious Business Name Registry

Your county clerk's office also usually administers your county's *fictitious business name registry.* When a business operates under a *fictitious business name* (a name different from a business owner's real name), it must register that name in the county in which it is located. The purpose of this registry is to enable the public to find the owner(s) of a business and to ensure that two businesses in the same area are not using the same name. You can use this registry to find any business your debtor may own and operate under a fictitious business name. You can usually search such a registry by the business name or by your debtor's name.

Tax Collector's Office

Your county *tax collector's office* is in charge of collecting property taxes and business taxes, and investigating delinquent revenue for your county. Your tax collector's office may help you find a business that your debtor owns, but has not registered anywhere else. Many people conduct business without registering their fictitious business name, but few conduct business without paying taxes.

Contractor Licensing Board

If your debtor is a contractor (someone who does construction, plumbing, painting, etc.), check with your state's *contractor licensing board* to see if he or she is licensed. If your debtor is licensed and the license is current, you will be able to get an address and a phone number. You may be able to get your debtor's contractor's license suspended if your judgment remains unsatisfied for a specified period of time.

WARNING

Suspending your debtor's contractor's license may actually do more harm than good. He or she may not have any other way to earn money to pay you, and the result is a catch-22. To avoid taking away your debtor's livelihood, you could make a deal with him or her to accept monthly payments. Both parties could agree to a payment schedule. The contractor could then submit the agreement to the licensing board to have the suspension lifted. If he or she then fails to make the payments per your agreement, you can notify the licensing board and have his or her license suspended again.

State Bar

Your *state bar* keeps records of all attorneys licensed to practice law in your state. If your debtor is or was a licensed attorney, check with your state bar to get a current or last known business address and phone number.

Court Files

Court files can be a wealth of information. Most court records are public information and are available for you to view. You would be surprised how much information you can get out of court files. You can find out if your debtor has been sued before, has sued anyone, changed his or her name, been divorced, adopted a child, etc.

If your debtor has ever been divorced (called a *dissolution of marriage*), you can review the family law files and look for a financial declaration. Even if the information is long outdated, it still might be useful. It might reveal what line of work your debtor is in or has done in the past. Similarly, if your debtor has children, he or she may have filed for child support or paid child support.

Locating Military Personnel

If the person you are trying to find is currently on active duty in the military, and you know his or her rank, name, and place where stationed, it is pretty easy to find him or her. You can usually locate such a debtor with a simple phone call.

If you know his or her full name, rank, and place where stationed, then do the following.

- Call long-distance information, and ask to be connected to the *base operator* at the military base in question. If you do not know which branch of the military your debtor is in, try them all.
- When the base operator comes on the line, ask to be connected to the base locator. The base locator can give you the duty phone number and duty address of any active duty person stationed on that base. Unless the individual has asked to keep the information private, the locator can also give you their home phone number and home address.
- If you are unsuccessful, look online at **www.militarylocator.com**.

If you do not know your debtor's rank or where he or she is stationed, then do the following.

- Contact the specific military service's member locator service (e.g., Navy, Air Force, Army, Marines, etc.). If you do not know which branch of the military your debtor is in, try them all.
- Give as much identifying information as possible about your debtor, such as full name, rank, last duty assignment/last known military address, service number, and Social Security number.

The locator service is free to immediate family members and government officials. Other family members, civilian friends, businesses, and others may be required to pay a fee. If so, the payment must be submitted by check or money order made out to the "U.S. Treasury," and is not refundable.

U.S. Army

The Army has no phone locator service. It also will not help in the location of retirees. Inquiries for all Army personnel should be mailed to:

Commander
U.S. Army Enlisted Records & Evaluation Center
ATTN: Locator
Fort Benjamin Harrison, IN 46249-5301

U.S. Navy

The Navy World Wide Locator helps locate individuals on active duty and those who have been recently discharged. The Navy also has a current address for retired Navy service members. Some addresses are protected under the provisions of the Privacy Act and cannot be released. Mail can be forwarded in those cases. You can call the locator service toll-free at 877-414-5359 or commercial 901-874-3388. Unless you are calling on official business or are a family member, the fee for researching an address is $3.50 or more per address, payable by check or money order to the U.S. Treasurer. Fees are retained in cases resulting in an unsuccessful search. Mail your correspondence with your fee (if applicable) to:

Navy World Wide Locator
Navy Personnel Command
PERS 312F
5720 Integrity Drive
Millington, TN 38055-3120

U.S. Air Force

The Air Force can locate active duty personnel, as well as retirees, reservists, and guardsmen. This information is not available for those who have separated from the Air Force or are Army Air Corps retirees. Information on individuals stationed overseas or in a sensitive position will not be released. However, the locator service will forward mail to that person for up to ninety days, as long as the correct postage is on the envelope and any required fee has been paid. Parents, spouses, and government officials may call 210-652-5774 for a recorded message or 210-652-5775 for non-recorded service.

HQ AFMPC/RMIQL

550 C Street, West
Suite 50
Randolph AFB, TX 78150-4752

The following information is required to make a positive identification:
- full name to include a middle initial;
- rank (officer/enlisted/GS);
- Social Security number or Air Force serial number; and,
- date of birth or an Air Force duty history to include the place, month, and year of assignments after June 1970. No assignment information is available prior to June 1970.

U.S. Marine Corps

The Marine Corps can provide the duty station for active duty personnel and reservists. For retired individuals, the locator service can provide the city and state, but not an address. The service will provide the service member's current rank and unit address; however, due to the locator's staffing, the office cannot forward mail except in special cases. Telephone requests to 703-784-3942 are free of charge to immediate family members and government officials calling on official business. In addition, telephone service will be provided at no cost to any individual, business, or organization, if the Marine locator decides the information would benefit the individual.

Commandant of the Marine Corps
Headquarters, USMC
Code MMSB-10
Quantico, VA 22134-5030

Coast Guard

The Coast Guard World Wide Locator can provide duty stations for active duty personnel. The telephone number is 202-372-8724.

If you are not able to locate your military debtor through the sources just covered, but you are sure he or she is in the military, hire a private detective to locate him or her. You can claim the investigator's fee as a cost of collecting your judgment by filing a Memorandum of Costs.

Internet

There are websites on the Internet that can help you find your missing debtor for a fee, usually under $50. It would be worth your time and money to use one of these websites before going to a private detective or giving up altogether and going to a judgment collector.

To find a website that will help you find your defendant, visit a popular search engine like **www.google.com** or **www.yahoo.com**, type in "missing person," visit some of the sites that pop up to see what you get for the fee, and then pick the one that seems the most comprehensive.

Secretary of State

Your secretary of state's office is usually the agency that governs business entities, such as corporations, limited liability companies, and limited partnerships. Your state may govern such business entities in an agency known as the *state corporation commission*. If you need a correct legal name, address, or agent for service of process for any of the business types mentioned above, contact the secretary of state, state corporation commission's office or your state's equivalent, or visit its website.

Alabama	www.sos.state.al.us
Alaska	www.dced.state.ak.us
Arizona	www.azsos.gov
Arkansas	www.sosweb.state.ar.us
California	www.sos.ca.gov
Colorado	www.sos.state.co.us
Connecticut	www.sots.state.ct.us
Delaware	www.sos.delaware.gov
Florida	www.dos.state.fl.us
Georgia	www.sos.state.ga.us
Hawaii	www.hawaii.gov/dcca/areas/breg
Idaho	www.idsos.state.id.us
Illinois	www.sos.state.il.us
Indiana	www.state.in.us/sos
Iowa	www.sos.state.ia.us
Kansas	www.kssos.org
Kentucky	www.sos.ky.gov
Louisiana	www.sec.state.la.us
Maine	www.state.me.us/sos
Maryland	www.sos.state.md.us
Massachusetts	www.state.ma.us/sec

Michigan	www.michigan.gov/sos
Minnesota	www.sos.state.mn.us
Mississippi	www.sos.state.ms.us
Missouri	www.sos.mo.gov
Montana	www.sos.state.mt.us/css
Nebraska	www.sos.state.ne.us
Nevada	www.sos.state.nv.us
New Hampshire	www.state.nh.us/sos
New Jersey	www.state.nj.us/state
New Mexico	www.sos.state.nm.us
New York	www.dos.state.ny.us
North Carolina	www.secstate.state.nc.us
North Dakota	www.nd.gov/sos
Ohio	www.sos.state.oh.us/sos
Oklahoma	www.sos.state.ok.us
Oregon	www.sos.state.or.us
Pennsylvania	www.dos.state.pa.us/dos
Rhode Island	www.state.ri.us
South Carolina	www.scsos.com
South Dakota	www.sdsos.gov
Tennessee	www.state.tn.us/sos
Texas	www.sos.state.tx.us
Utah	www.commerce.state.ut.us
Vermont	www.sec.state.vt.us
Virginia	www.soc.state.va.us
Washington	www.secstate.wa.gov
West Virginia	www.wvsos.com
Wisconsin	www.sos.state.wi.us
Wyoming	http://soswy.state.wy.us

For any other information about an LLC, LP, or LLP, you will probably have to submit your questions in writing to your secretary of state's office, state corporation commission, or your state's equivalent.

DECEASED DEBTOR

If you suspect your debtor may have died and left any property (called an *estate*), check the court's *probate* files in the county where he or she died or where he or she lived at the time of death. If your debtor had a *small estate* (not very many assets), there may not be a case in probate. In most states, estates under a certain dollar amount do not have to go through probate. If you do find out that your debtor has died, you will have to continue your collection efforts in another way. If your debtor's estate is large enough (some states require a minimum dollar amount of $100,000) to have to be *admitted* (filed) in probate court, then you would file a claim with the court the deceased debtor's case is in, against his or her estate. That is called a *creditor's claim.*

Most states have a specific time period in which creditors must file claims in order to collect from a deceased debtor's estate. Usually, the executor of your debtor's estate must publish notice of a probate proceeding so that creditors have a fair chance of finding out about the death and filing a claim. Check local newspapers (including legal notice papers) in the area you think your debtor lived in to look for such notice, and be sure to file your claim on time.

If your debtor's estate is less than the amount required to file in probate, it will probably be very difficult to collect your money. In such a situation, your debtor's assets will probably be transferred directly to his or her *heirs* (those people either designated by your debtor to receive his or her assets or those legally in line to receive your debtor's assets). Call your debtor's next of kin and ask about the distribution of your debtor's assets. It is likely you will be told there is nothing left. You will have to make a decision at this point. If you want to continue, you will have to do additional research into collection laws that are not covered in this book. Investigate how to go after assets in an estate that has already passed to your debtor's heirs, or take a tax write-off for your loss and put the entire thing behind you.

DEBTOR WHO HAS LEFT THE STATE

If your debtor moved to a different state, you can *transfer* your judgment to that new state and enforce it against your debtor's assets there.

You may either register your judgment as a *sister-state judgment* (called that because all fifty states recognize the judgments of all other states) in the new state (called *domesticating* your judgment), or initiate an entirely new civil case on the underlying debt or injury, which means suing your debtor all over again in the new state. However, you cannot do both. You cannot be in the process of enforcing your judgment and simultaneously file and pursue a civil case on that same judgment. You need to select one method of collection—either domesticate your judgment or initiate a civil action. Due to the high cost of litigation, domesticating your judgment will be the least expensive approach.

Sister-State Judgment

To collect your judgment entered by a court in your state against your debtor now living in another state, you have to first turn your judgment into a judgment of that new state. For example, if you got your judgment in Florida and then your debtor moved to California, you would have to turn your Florida judgment into a California judgment before you could enforce it in California. When you are transferring your judgment to another state, you are trying to domesticate a sister-state judgment. A judgment entered in a different state than the state in which you want to enforce it is considered a sister-state judgment.

A sister-state judgment must be domesticated before it can be enforced in a new state. You will not be able to get a writ or put a lien on any property without domesticating your judgment first. To domesticate a sister-state judgment, you need to find out what the new state requires. Most states make you fill out a form, file it, and send your debtor a copy. After a designated period of time passes, your judgment is domesticated and you can start to collect it.

To find out a particular state's procedures, access that state's website or visit a courthouse and see if an advisor or clerk is available to assist you. If you want to do it on your own, look for the relevant law in that state's code of civil procedure; look in the index under "judgment enforcement." The law will probably treat money judgments and non-money judgments differently. Make sure you are following the law that relates to *money judgments*. Once you have completed domesticating your judgment, collect it as if it had been a judgment entered originally in your state.

Consider all of the expenses you will incur before starting the domestication process. If your debtor still has assets left in the state in which your judgment was originally entered and you know where those assets are located, then hold off on domesticating your judgment in a new state and proceed against the assets and not the debtor.

To have a sister-state judgment domesticated, do the following.

- Determine which court would be a proper venue in which to domesticate your judgment. You need to file it in the county where your debtor lives, or in any county if the defendant is a nonresident.
- Check with the clerk of the court if a form is available for this process.
- Get an authenticated/certified copy of your judgment from the court that entered it.
- File the form and the filing fee with the clerk, who will then enter the judgment. Be sure to acknowledge the interest that has accrued, using the applicable rate from the state that entered your judgment. Once your new judgment is entered, it begins to accrue interest at the applicable rate for that new state.
- After your judgment is entered, you will need to serve your debtor notice of the domestication. Check with the clerk of the court to see if a proof of service form is available.
- After you have someone serve your debtor notice, you must file a proof of service with the new court.

There will probably be a *stay of enforcement* or *stay of execution* ordered after your new judgment is entered. For the prescribed number of days, you will be restricted in what you can do to collect your money. Also, if there is a stay of enforcement or stay of execution ordered in the state that originally entered your judgment, then your judgment cannot be enforced in any other state until the stay is either lifted or expires. The purpose of the stay is to give your debtor the opportunity to challenge the domestication of the judgment.

When a stay of enforcement has been ordered, that usually means you may not take any steps to collect your judgment, while a stay of execution usually means you may not use a *writ of execution* to initiate any collection procedures.

It may be possible to start collection procedures before the notice is sent and the stay of execution or enforcement expires, but you would have to get court approval. Getting court approval may be as easy as marking a box on the application form. In situations where you would be greatly harmed if not permitted to enforce your judgment immediately, the court may order that you be able to move ahead before the expiration of the stay of execution or enforcement. An example of such a situation would be if your debtor is holding a voluntary liquidation sale in the next month and getting rid of his or her property.

MOTION TO VACATE

A *motion* is a request to the court to do something. A *motion to vacate* is a request by a debtor to the court to kick out your judgment (the judgment that you just domesticated). The grounds for a successful motion to vacate will vary from state to state.

A motion to vacate can also be filed to correct the accrued interest on your judgment. Do not worry—the court will not kick out your old judgment and leave you with no judgment at all based only on a miscalculation of interest. The old judgment would be vacated and a new judgment with the correct interest would be entered. If your debtor files a motion to vacate, another stay of execution or stay of enforcement is ordered until the motion is heard.

To oppose a debtor's motion to vacate your judgment, do the following:

- draft an *opposition to judgment debtor's motion to vacate* on pleading paper (see Chapter 10);
- make at least three copies;
- file a copy with the court;
- have someone serve your debtor a copy;
- file a proof of service with the court;
- attend the hearing that is scheduled on your debtor's motion; and,
- argue to the court why your debtor's motion should be denied.

If you need guidance on a sample opposition to judgment debtor's motion to vacate, consult a practice guide or a forms guide in your local law library. Also, check the court's local rules to find out if you need to serve your opposition and file the original with a proof of service or if you file it first and then serve it.

PRIVATE INVESTIGATOR

If you are still not able to find your debtor, consider hiring a private investigator. If you decide to take this route, call several private investigators and ask for a price quote. Whatever you do, do not hire someone on an hourly rate. *Always* negotiate a flat fee.

4

Debtor Examination Hearings

In a *debtor examination hearing,* you *examine* (question) your debtor at the courthouse about what assets he or she owns and where they are located. You may also examine a *third party* (someone not named on the judgment) who has information about your debtor's finances, owes your debtor money, or is in possession of your debtor's property.

Debtor examination hearings are called different names in different juris-dictions. You may hear the term "OEX" when referring to debtor exami-nations; this stands for an *order to appear for examination.* You can refer to your local court rules to find out what your jurisdiction calls its debtor examinations. Some of the more common names are *citation to discover assets, financial disclosure statement, disclosure hearing, debtor rule examina-tion,* and *subpoena and affidavit for judgment debtor examination.*

In addition to referring to your local rules, you can also check a practice guide in your local law library to find out what to call a debtor examination in your court.

EXAMPLES OF STATE-SPECIFIC REQUIREMENTS

In Hawaii, to examine your debtor, you would file an ex parte motion for an examination of your judgment debtor. The same form also works for examining a third person who holds money or property belonging to your debtor.

In Wisconsin, your debtor is sent a statement of assets form as soon as the judgment is entered. A *statement of assets* is a financial statement to be completed by your debtor and mailed directly back to you. Your debtor has fifteen days to send the statement of assets to you, unless an appeal is filed or he or she has asked the court for an order delaying that fifteen-day due date. Otherwise, you could file a motion and order for contempt. If your debtor failed to attend the hearing on the motion for contempt, the court could issue a bench warrant for your debtor's arrest. If he or she does show up to the hearing, the court would order him or her to complete the statement of assets right there in court.

In Georgia, you are *not* permitted to go straight to an examination hearing. You must first have the court clerk send your debtor *interrogatories* (written questions) by certified mail. If your debtor fails to *answer* (file a response to the examination questions) within thirty days, you then file a motion to get a hearing to require an answer to the interrogatories form.

In New Jersey, the process is similar to the process in Georgia. You need to first send your debtor an information subpoena, which is a form of interrogatories that he or she has twenty-one days to answer. You have to have someone serve him or her by personal service or by certified mail. If your debtor does not respond, you may then ask the court for permission to send interrogatories to a third party who may owe your defendant money or possess anything of value owned by your defendant.

In Kentucky, as in New Jersey and Georgia, you are required to send your debtor written interrogatories. (Refer to a practice guide for sample interrogatories.) Your debtor then has thirty days to answer. If he or she fails to do so, you have to file a post-judgment motion/order requiring him or her to answer your interrogatories.

If your state does not require you to first send your debtor interrogatories, proceed directly to a debtor examination hearing.

It is very possible that your court may call its debtor examinations something completely different and even require you to follow more or fewer steps than covered here. Keep your focus on the big picture—understand the overall process before you file for a debtor examination, whatever that process may be called.

SCHEDULING AN EXAMINATION

To file for an examination hearing, get the required forms from your court clerk's office. Your local court rules will tell you on which days of the week your courthouse holds examination hearings, in which room (sometimes called *department*) you should appear, and how to file the forms. You may have to pick a date for your hearing, write it on your documents, and file them with the court clerk before you serve the other party. Or you may have to do just the opposite—pick a date for your hearing, write it on your documents, serve the party, and then file your papers. If standardized forms are available, read them carefully before completing them.

WHERE TO FILE

Check to see if there are restrictions concerning where your debtor currently lives and in which courthouse your examination hearing must be held. For example, it may be required that your examination hearing be held at a courthouse within a certain number miles of where your debtor currently lives. If your debtor has moved outside that specified distance from your courthouse, then you will have to hold your examination in a courthouse closer to where your debtor lives now. If you end up having to go to another courthouse, check the local rules of that courthouse for the requirements. Again, try to look up the rules for that new courthouse online before going down to your local law library.

IF YOUR DEBTOR HAS MOVED

In most states, if your debtor moved to another county in your state, all you need to do is get a certified copy of your judgment or an abstract of judgment from the court that entered your judgment. Take your abstract (once issued by the court) or your certified copy of your judgment to the courthouse closest to your debtor's new home and file for a debtor's examination hearing. Inform the clerk why you are filing for an examination hearing in a different court. You will probably be given a different case number to be used just for that examination hearing. You will resume use of your original case number for every other procedure in your courthouse after that hearing.

WHO TO EXAMINE

You can examine your debtor and anyone else who owes your debtor money, controls your debtor's property, or has knowledge of your debtor's assets. As mentioned earlier, some states require that you examine your debtor first before examining a third party, but you may be allowed to skip examining your debtor and go directly to examining a third party if you have *cause* (a good reason).

FORMS

If you are going to examine someone other than your debtor, you will need to either fill out forms for a third-party examination or note on the form that you are examining a third party. If your debtor is a corporation, LP, or LLC, you will always be examining a third party (because those businesses are entities and not human beings), such as the company's chief executive officer (CEO) or chief financial officer (CFO). (See examples of examination hearings forms in Appendix B.)

Copies

Your local rules will also tell you how many copies of your forms you must file. Also, note whether the forms can be handwritten or whether they must be typed. When in doubt, type the forms. Take at least three copies with you along with the original; one copy for your debtor, one copy for you, one spare, and the original for the court. Again, first find out if you need to file first and then serve your debtor or serve your debtor first and then file your paperwork.

SCHEDULING A TIME

Before you schedule your hearing date, you will need to find out how many days' *notice* you must give your debtor (meaning how long you have to serve your debtor the paperwork before the hearing). Be sure that you schedule your hearing far enough in the future that you allow yourself enough time to have your debtor served.

In some courts, debtor exams are held every day at the same time. If this is the case in your courthouse, just select a day that will give you enough time to serve your debtor with the required notice and that is good for your schedule. You must then have your debtor personally served with the debtor's copy so he or she knows when and where to come to court. Whoever serves your debtor needs to complete a proof of service and return it to you. Return the proof of service and a copy of your paperwork to the clerk's office. (For more information on service of process, see page 23.)

In some states, the clerk does all the scheduling. You just need to complete the required form and turn it in with the required number of copies, and the clerk will take it from there.

SERVICE OF YOUR PAPERS

In some states, you can have a friend serve your examination paperwork to your debtor, but in many states, you need to have a process server, the sheriff's department, or marshall serve your paperwork. If your debtor does not show up to your first scheduled hearing, the clerk will probably reschedule your hearing and send your debtor a threatening letter, sometimes called a *bench letter.*

In some states, like Maine, you do not have to go through the bench letter step. If your debtor does not show up to your first scheduled hearing, you complete an affidavit and request for a civil order for arrest. You have to pay a fee and the sheriff will go out and pick up your debtor and bring him or her to court.

In states that do not send a bench letter, the court will probably only issue a bench warrant for your debtor's arrest if he or she is served properly by a process server, the sheriff's department, or a marshall. A *bench warrant* is an arrest warrant issued by a judge instructing the sheriff's department to go out and pick up your debtor. Your debtor will not end up sitting in jail—he or she will be picked up and brought to the courthouse to set bail. However, if you had your debtor served by someone other than a sheriff's deputy, a process server, or a marshall, the court probably will not issue a bench warrant.

If your debtor is picked up on a bench warrant and posts bail to get out, you can get the court to order that bail money handed over to you. Check with the clerk who issues the bench warrants for the specific requirements in your court. (You may need a turnover order. See page 130 for more information on turnover orders.)

(See Appendix C for a sample debtor examination form.)

SUBPOENAS

It is a good idea to have your debtor bring his or her financial records to your examination hearing. Most debtors will not voluntarily bring their personal financial papers, so you will have to subpoena them. A *subpoena* is a court order that orders someone to appear in court. A *subpoena duces tecum* is an order to appear in court and bring specific documents to the court. It will be much easier to conduct your debtor exam if your debtor brings his or her financial records, such as bank account statements and tax returns, to court. It really is worth your time to file a subpoena duces tecum and have it served on your debtor with your examination hearing papers. It will only take a few extra minutes to fill out a subpoena and file it. It may even scare your debtor into voluntarily paying you. (See Appendix C for a sample subpoena duces tecum.)

When completing the form for a subpoena duces tecum, be as thorough as possible. Request every document that you suspect will reveal relevant information concerning your debtor's financial affairs. Keep in mind that any money owed to your debtor from a third party should also be investigated during your examination hearing and when completing your subpoena. If there are any documents that your debtor has that may lead to information concerning any assets of which your debtor or a third party has possession, request them in your subpoena.

Once your paperwork is filed and served to your debtor (or served to your debtor and then filed, whichever process is required in your state), you can start preparing for your examination hearing.

THE HEARING

Due to the private nature of the information revealed in debtor exams, the hearings are conducted very differently from trials. There will probably only be a few people in the courtroom. In most states, you will not be conducting your examination in front of a judge or commissioner. Usually, the court clerk swears you both in and then instructs you to go off to the side to examine your debtor. Find a comfortable place to sit and get going.

In Maine, debtor examinations are conducted a little differently. A judge will be present to oversee your examination and both parties may subpoena witnesses. After you complete your examination, the judge will make a decision about how your debtor should pay you and when.

UNCOOPERATIVE DEBTOR

Unfortunately, not all things go as planned. If your debtor fails to produce any of the documents that you subpoenaed or to answer your questions, instruct your debtor that he or she may be held in contempt. If your debtor then agrees to produce the documents at a later date, you can ask the clerk to reschedule your hearing. You can also proceed with your examination and inform the clerk that you need an additional date on the calendar for your debtor to produce the documents that he or she failed to bring.

If your debtor still refuses to answer your questions or promise to produce the documents that you requested at a later date, again ask the clerk for assistance from the judicial officer in charge of debtor exams. Hopefully, the judicial officer assigned to the examination calendar will take the bench and instruct your debtor to cooperate, or will conduct your exam for you.

TIPS FOR CONDUCTING YOUR EXAMINATION

If you were nervous about appearing in court for your trial, then you may want to attend a few examination hearings before actually conducting one of your own. Call your courthouse or look in your court's local rules to get the time and location for debtor examinations. Due to the private nature of the information revealed, you will probably only be able to observe from a distance.

Review the *Individual Debtor Examination Questionnaire* in Appendix D. Add questions that are specific to your debtor and omit questions that do not apply to him or her. Bring your debtor questionnaire to the hearing, along with several pens and some paper. Bring a turnover order. Have everything filled in but the specific property that you want the court to turn over, which you can fill in if and when your debtor reveals he or she is currently carrying cash. Bring three copies.

Start your examination by setting the ground rules with your debtor. Always be professional. Look your debtor in the eye and say, "Hello. We'll start by you completing this questionnaire. When you are done, I'll ask you some questions about your assets. While answering the questionnaire and my follow-up questions, be as thorough as possible. Do you have any questions before we begin?" You control the examination. Do not allow your debtor to run over you.

Stay focused! Do not allow yourself to be sidetracked. This is not the time to discuss the underlying merits of your case—that time has passed. You now have a judgment and that is all that matters. If your debtor persists, say, "I'm attempting to collect the judgment the court has ordered. If I need assistance conducting this examination, I can request the commissioner/judge take the bench and order you to answer, if you would prefer." If your debtor continues to be difficult, ask him or her to stay seated while you go to the courtroom clerk and ask for the commissioner/judge's help. Explain your debtor's behavior and ask for help.

Before you start asking questions, take a look at your debtor's key chain. Ask your debtor to show you his or her keys, and then ask what each key goes to. If it is a car, ask the make, model, year, and who owns it. If one of the keys goes to a house or a commercial building, ask who the owner is and where it is located. If the debtor denies ownership of the item for which he or she has a key, then ask why he or she has a key to something he or she does not own. Does it belong to the debtor's employer? Who is his or her employer?

Hand your debtor the examination questionnaire and wait patiently for him or her to complete it. Do not be surprised if he or she makes comments or fails to complete it. Simply review it when your debtor is done and go through it question by question. Ask follow-up questions.

Next, ask if your debtor owns or is owed anything valuable that you have not mentioned or covered. If you do not get a straight answer, rephrase your question and ask it at a later time in the examination.

You do not want to dive right in and ask your debtor, "Wher [ ] bank?" Your debtor will understand the significance of this que [ ] run right out after the examination hearing to close accounts. Bury the question about your debtor's bank account information in the middle of other questions. Make the question about his or her bank account seem insignificant so that you do not draw attention to the issue. If you do find out about a bank account, then immediately after completing your debtor's examination, go to the clerk's office to get a writ. When you have a writ, go directly to the levying officer and get a bank levy.

Finally, ask the debtor if he or she has any cash. If the answer is yes, ask how much. If your debtor does have some cash, then you need to make a decision. You can ask the court for a turnover order for your debtor to turn the cash over to you, or you can let it go. There are two schools of thought on this. Of course, if your debtor has $2,000 on him or her, have it ordered turned over. However, it is more likely that he or she will have $50 or less in cash. Do you take it? Some courts dislike turnover orders, so it might be a battle to have a commissioner/judge sign your order. You would probably be better off telling your debtor "I'll let you keep that to get home and get something to eat, but that is it."

EXAMINATION LIENS

Once the paperwork for your examination hearing is served, a *lien* is usually established on all of your debtor's personal property (some say the lien is established at the time the paperwork is filed). This lien can last up to a year. A lien puts a hold on your debtor's property and prohibits him or her from transferring that property to someone else. If your debtor does transfer the property, you would then have a case to have that sale cancelled and that property seized, which is beyond the scope of this book. If you find yourself in this situation, do additional research.

BUSINESS DEBTOR EXAMINATION

If your judgment is against a business and not an individual (even if the business is a sole proprietorship), you should have your debtor complete the *Business Debtor Examination Questionnaire.* (see Appendix D.) When conducting an examination of a business debtor, you must pay close attention to who owns each asset discussed. Are the assets in the name of the business itself or in the name of the business owner?

If the name on your judgment is only the name of the business, then you should look for assets that are in that very same name. Be careful not to be fooled with property that is being leased. Anything being leased is out of reach, because leased property is actually owned by another party and is only being rented by your debtor. Clearly ask your debtor if each asset mentioned or identified in the questionnaire is owned or leased. If your debtor says that a particular asset is owned but not paid off, then follow up and find out how much, if any, is still owed on it, and to whom.

As previously mentioned, do not let your debtor intimidate you. The business employee or owner may try to stonewall you or act aloof, but do not let it last long. If you are not able to gain control of your examination hearing, tell your debtor that you need to take a break. If, after you return from a break, you can still not gain control of your examination, then go to the court clerk and arrange for you and your debtor to immediately appear in front of a commissioner/judge.

> ## ⚠ WARNING
>
> When a judicial officer is forced to take the bench and help you question your debtor, he or she is not going to be very happy about it. Only resort to this tactic when you are truly having trouble.

TIME LIMITS

Check your local rules of court for the parameters of your debtor exam. If you are not able to find the answer, ask the courtroom clerk. Take your time questioning your debtor, because in most jurisdictions, you may only conduct a debtor examination every couple of months. If you conclude your examination hearing prematurely, you are out of luck. You will have to wait it out or file a motion requesting permission to conduct another hearing without having to wait.

ALTERNATIVES TO A DEBTOR EXAMINATION

If you do not want to conduct a debtor exam, you might be able to send your debtor written interrogatories. Check your local rules to see if you are permitted to use interrogatories instead of holding a debtor exam. If you are, be sure to check how many interrogatories you may send and how often you may send them. Also, be sure to clarify whether a question with sub-parts counts as one question or several questions. *Written interrogatories* require written responses from your debtor done under *oath* (where your debtor signs at the bottom of the page swearing that he or she told the truth in his or her responses).

There is clearly a downside to using written interrogatories instead of conducting an in-person debtor's exam. If you send your debtor interrogatories, you are not able to immediately ask follow-up questions, as you would if your debtor was sitting right in front of you. Another problem you will face with interrogatories is that they give your debtor more advance notice that you are coming after his or her assets.

It is up to you and your level of comfort in deciding which method you use to elicit information from your debtor. If you really do not want to see your debtor again, then look into sending interrogatories. Whichever method you end up using, make sure you are thorough. Do not rush it. If you decide to conduct a debtor examination, do not wrap up your exam until you have exhausted every question.

If you are still not able to get any information concerning the existence and location of assets owned by or owed to your debtor, you will need to choose among the following options.

- Walk away from your judgment for now. Let it earn interest for a few years. Try to collect it again after your debtor has had some time to earn some money or purchase property.
- Have a private detective or asset search company do an asset search on your debtor. If you decide to have an asset search done, add the cost to your judgment by filing a Memorandum of Costs.
- Assign your judgment to a judgment collection professional. You can expect to pay up to 50% of your judgment in fees, although this percentage is usually negotiable. You do not have to pay up front. The collector is only paid if he or she is able to collect your money.

STEP 3

COLLECTION PROCEDURES

5

Prepare for Collection

Once you have located your debtor's assets, you will need to understand the procedures that you will use to turn those assets into money. As mentioned earlier, each state has its own procedural laws, so it is possible that your state may prohibit one or more of the procedures that will be covered in this section or require that it be carried out differently. Verify whether a procedure is available in your state and what steps you need to follow before beginning.

As you read through Step 3, keep your focus on the big picture. Your state's rules for a particular collection procedure may be a little different, so this book does not focus exclusively on the names of individual procedures. Instead, focus on the idea. For example, you will learn that you can get the money in your debtor's bank account. Do not fixate on the names *bank levy* and *writ of execution*. Your state may refer to the process as a *garnishment* and require you to get a *writ of garnishment*. It is more important that you understand that the process is available to you, whatever it may be called in your state.

Keep track of your expenses and be sure to add them to your judgment as soon as possible. In most states, you may add all reasonable costs you incur while attempting to collect your judgment to your judgment by filing a Memorandum of Costs (or your state's equivalent) with the court within a certain amount of time from when the costs are incurred. For example, in California costs must be added to your judgment within two years of incurring the cost.

CERTIFYING YOUR JUDGMENT

Connecticut, the District of Columbia, New Jersey, South Carolina, Minnesota, Washington, and Texas all require some form of certification of your judgment before you begin to collect.

For example, in Connecticut, you are required to fill out a Satisfaction of Judgment—Non-Payment form. Once this form is filed with the court, your judgment is entered into the court's *docket* (record book). The court generates an order of execution. You then take that to the levying officer (the sheriff) and proceed to go after your debtor's assets.

In South Carolina, you start by recording your judgment with the clerk of court.

In New Jersey, the form you need to file is called a Statement of Docketing.

In Texas, you certify your judgment by filing an abstract of judgment with the court clerk; doing so also establishes a lien on any real property your debtor owns.

Before beginning collections, check with the clerk of your court to ask whether certifying your judgment is required. If the clerk has no idea what you are talking about, the answer is probably no. If your court does not require that you certify your judgment first, proceed to the instructions to file an abstract of judgment.

ABSTRACT OF JUDGMENT

An *abstract of judgment* is an important tool to help you collect your judgment. It may also be called a *memorandum of judgment, certificate of judgment,* or *lien certificate.* Getting an abstract of judgment, or your state's equivalent, is a simple and inexpensive process. Abstracts are used to place liens on real and personal property. A lien is a method to secure your judgment by attaching it to the title of a piece of personal property or a piece of real property (real estate).

An abstract of judgment can secure your judgment against a bankruptcy, should one occur. File an abstract of judgment with the court that entered your judgment and file an original abstract in every county that you know or suspect your debtor has any interest in real property, or will get any interest in real property. Even if your debtor does not own any real property today, he or she might buy something in a few years. If you have filed an abstract of judgment with the recorder's office in a county in which your debtor has any interest in real property, a lien will be placed on that property. Also, if your debtor acquires property after you have recorded an abstract, a lien will be established as to the new property.

To have an abstract of judgment issued, do the following:

- get the appropriate form(s) from the court that entered your judgment;
- complete the form(s) and file them with the clerk;
- pay the appropriate filing fee(s); and,
- file an original abstract of judgment at the recorder's office in each county in which you think your debtor may have real property.

(See a sample Abstract of Judgment in Appendix C.)

Debtor with Multiple Names

If your debtor goes by different names, you will have to file an additional document, sometimes called an affidavit of identity, to have the extra names added to your abstract of judgment. An *affidavit of identity* is a document that you may need to draft and file with the court at the same time you get an abstract of judgment issued in order to identify additional names— aliases—that your debtor uses. **This is not a way to add additional debtors to your judgment.**

Filing an affidavit of identity is a good idea in any case in which your debtor uses different names or different spellings of his or her name. In your affidavit, you must provide sufficient facts to establish that the additional name you are providing to the court is actually used by your debtor and is not an additional debtor. The court must approve your affidavit before the clerk can issue an abstract of judgment with your debtor's additional name.

Recording an Abstract of Judgment

To *record* an abstract of judgment simply means to file it with the recorder-assessor's office in each county in which your debtor has or will have any real property. Defects in the recordation of your abstract, such as a misspelled name or an omission of requested information, can nullify and render ineffective any lien established, so you should provide as much information about your debtor as you can.

6

Liens

A *lien* is a method to secure your judgment by attaching it to the title of a piece of personal property or a piece of real property (real estate). You can place a lien on any of the debtor's real or personal property.

REAL PROPERTY LIENS

A lien on *real property* will secure your judgment against a bankruptcy. It is a good idea to create a lien on any interest in real property your debtor has or will have in the future. Keep in mind that establishing a real property lien will probably not produce any cash, unless the property on which you have established a lien is refinanced or sold. Your judgment will then have to be paid first.

It is good practice to immediately record an original abstract of judgment in each county in which you think your debtor owns or will own real property. You will have to fill out a request form and pay a separate filing fee for each original that you have issued. Be sure to provide all the information that you have about your debtor when completing the form.

In states like Wisconsin, all you need to do is *register* (or sometimes *certify*) your judgment with the court to place a lien on all real property owned in that county by your debtor. If you want to put a lien on real property owned by your debtor in a different county in Wisconsin than the county that entered your judgment, you would need to get a certified copy of your judgment and register it with the court in the new county. That court would then enter your judgment into its docket.

PERSONAL PROPERTY LIENS

In addition to placing a lien on any real property your debtor owns, you should also consider filing an abstract of judgment with your secretary of state to create a lien on any of your debtor's *personal property* as well.

Placing a lien on personal property of individual debtors and business debtors is another method to collect your judgment. However, it is not a method that will likely produce any money by itself, unless your debtor voluntarily pays you to have the lien removed.

The purpose of placing a lien on personal property is to prevent that property from being sold. In some cases, it may also secure your judgment if your debtor files bankruptcy. Placing such a lien gives you and your judgment priority over most liens filed after yours. It also serves to put others on *constructive notice* of your lien. For example, if someone purchases the property from your debtor after an abstract has been filed, they did so with notice of your lien, so you would have a good argument to get that property back.

Not all personal property is subject to judgment liens. Property that is typically not subject to a judgment lien on personal property includes:

- vehicles;
- vessels;
- mobile homes;
- property that is a fixture in real property (attached to the property); and,
- inventory items with a unit price of less than $500 (business debtors).

To file a judgment lien on personal property, do the following.

- Get the forms for an abstract of judgment or your state's equivalent from the court that entered your judgment.
- Complete the forms and file them with the clerk of the court that entered your judgment.
- Pay the appropriate filing fee (usually about $15).
- Get the form for a notice of a judgment lien, or your state's equivalent. If there is not a form, contact the secretary of state's office for instructions on what is needed.
- Complete the form.
- File it with the secretary of state's office with the abstract of judgment. The fee may be added to your judgment as an enforcement cost.
- Serve your debtor. Pay the filing fee.

Service of the notice to your debtor can probably be done by mail or in person. Check your state for its service requirements. If your judgment was ordered to be paid in installment payments, you probably cannot file a lien on personal property. Check with your court for details.

For further instructions about adding costs to your judgment, see the "Crediting Payments Received" section on page 16.

Judgment liens on personal property only last for a few years (for example, five years in California). Also, this type of lien can usually not be renewed. Therefore, it is essential to try to collect your judgment within the designated time period before your lien expires. Judgment liens on real property, on the other hand, usually last until your judgment is either satisfied in full or expires.

As with most liens, the first lien established usually has priority. There are exceptions to the "first in time, first in line" rule, as there are in almost every area of the law. As a general rule, judgment liens for child support and IRS liens will always take priority over other judgment liens from civil judgments.

Once you have recorded an abstract of judgment, you can proceed to the more aggressive collection procedures. Remember to keep track of your fees and periodically add them to your judgment.

To add the fees to your judgment, do the following.

- Complete a Memorandum of Costs, or your state's equivalent.
- Make a copy.
- Have someone serve your debtor the copy (probably by mail).
- Have the person who served your debtor complete a proof of service form.
- Return the original Memorandum of Costs form with a completed proof of service to the court that entered your judgment.

After every collection procedure, follow the instructions above to add the fees you have paid to your judgment.

NOTICE OF LIENS

Your debtor must be notified of any liens established. You may serve your debtor with a notice and file a proof of service with the office that established the lien or have that office send a notice to your debtor for you. If you are charged a fee for service of your notice, you may add that fee to the lien, but that cost usually must not exceed what it would cost the office to send it. Use the method of service that is the least expensive.

LIFE OF LIENS

A judgment lien on real property will usually last the life of your judgment, unless your judgment is satisfied or you voluntarily release it. A lien on real property can be extended if your judgment is renewed for an additional period of time. In most states, all you need to do to extend your lien is record your application for the renewal of your judgment with the recorder-assessor's office in each county in which you filed an abstract. Verify this procedure with the recorder-assessor's office when you record your abstract.

LIEN FROM SISTER-STATE JUDGMENT

When a sister-state judgment is domesticated in a new state, it is treated just like any other judgment entered in that new state. If the new state requires that an abstract of judgment (or its equivalent document) be issued and recorded to establish a lien on real property, then do so with your sister-state judgment after it has been domesticated.

CO-OWNED PROPERTY

You can place a lien on property that is owned by your debtor and another party as long as your debtor's name is on title to that property. Title to property can be *held,* or owned, in different ways. Just as a pie can be cut into a few pieces or many pieces, ownership of property can be divided in the same way.

One way to hold title to property is as *joint tenants with the right of survivorship,* which means if one owner dies, his or her interest in the property goes to the other owners and not to his or her estate. People can also own property together as *tenants in common,* which means if one owner dies, his or her interest passes to his or her estate and not to the other owner.

Property that is owned in joint tenancy with the right of survivorship can have a lien attached, but the lien does not survive if the debtor passes away. Your lien will not pass with the property to the other joint tenant; it will be extinguished.

If the property is owned as tenants in common, your lien will survive your debtor's death. If a co-tenant dies, that tenant's interest in the property does not pass to the other tenants—it passes to the deceased tenant's estate. Therefore, your lien would survive your debtor's death and remain with the property.

Also, in a *community property* state (a state that deems each partner in a marriage, or domestic partnership in some states, to own an undivided share of all marital property), if a lien is placed on property owned by a married couple, and only one member of the couple is your debtor, the lien still attaches to the entire piece of property.

TRANSFER OF PROPERTY

Property subject to a lien will usually not transfer to another owner without the lien being paid first. Any prospective buyer would want the property delivered free of any liens. However, if your debtor transfers his or her property to a family member or friend, your lien will probably not be paid at the time of transfer.

If your debtor does *transfer* (sell or give away) his or her property after you have created your lien, the property transfers with your lien attached, regardless of the form of ownership. It is as if the transfer never took place. The *transferee* (the one receiving the property) is deemed to have constructive notice of your lien and takes the property subject to your lien.

If there is more than one lien on a piece of property, preexisting liens are said to have priority over newly placed liens. Liens that are established first are known as *senior* liens and those that are filed after are considered *junior* liens. When an owner of property, or any other party, attempts to remove liens, senior liens are paid first, then junior liens.

OUTCOME OF A LIEN

Placing a judgment lien on real property will probably not produce any money, unless your debtor voluntarily pays you or the property is sold or refinanced. To produce any money, you will have to force the sale of the property, which is a process too costly to make it worthwhile unless your judgment is for a significant amount. For example, it would not be cost effective to try to force the sale of a home to satisfy a $5,000 judgment, but if your judgment is for $100,000, it would certainly be worth the time and fees you will have to spend to force the sale of your debtor's property.

Forcing the sale of real property to collect a judgment is beyond the scope of this book. Consult an attorney if you wish to force the sale of your debtor's home.

Otherwise, the purpose of your lien is to secure your judgment and to save your place in line just in case your debtor transfers the property or refinances it.

RELEASING A LIEN BEFORE YOUR JUDGMENT IS PAID

If your debtor's property is the only substantial asset he or she owns, he or she may want to refinance it or borrow against it to pay you off. To do so, you would need to subordinate your lien to the new lender's lien.

Subordinating a lien to another lien means allowing another lien to take your place in line. You are not getting out of line; you are just allowing someone to cut in front of you. Your senior lien becomes a junior lien to the one you are allowing to cut in front of you. You may be asked to sign a release to allow this to happen. **Be sure not to give a general release of claim.** It is also a good practice to specify the property in question in any agreement you enter.

If you are asked to allow another lien to take your place, require your debtor to draft the agreement. Review the agreement thoroughly to make sure you are not signing away your right in line behind the new senior lien. If you have questions or concerns about any document you are asked to sign, contact an attorney.

RELEASING A LIEN AFTER YOUR JUDGMEN

If your judgment has been satisfied, you are required to fil
edgment of satisfaction of judgment, or your state's equivalent, ..
that entered your judgment.

If you fail to notify the court that your judgment has been satisfied, you
could become liable to your debtor for any damages that result. If you
established a judgment lien on your debtor's property, you must notify
your debtor and inform him or her of the counties in which you recorded
an abstract of judgment. It is then up to your debtor to file a certified copy
of the satisfaction of judgment with that county's recorder-assessor's office.
Check the procedural law in your jurisdiction to make sure that it is your
debtor's responsibility to have any judgment liens released.

Writs

A *writ* is an order issued by the court that entered your judgment. It gives permission to the levying officer, usually the sheriff's department, to start a collection procedure to collect your judgment. Think of a writ like the permission slip you used to get signed by your parents for field trips from school. You would fill most of it out and give it to your parents to sign. Once it was signed, you would give it to your teacher and you would be allowed to go on the field trip. Writs are pretty similar. You complete the form, turn it in to the court that entered your judgment for a "signature," and take it to the levying officer to start a collection procedure.

Many judgment creditors know they need to get a writ, but they are not quite sure what to do with it once they get it. Some people know to take it to the sheriff's office, but do not fully understand why. Once at the sheriff's office, you will be asked, "What do you want us to do?" When you reply, "Get my money," they may ask you, "How?" You can see how frustrating a conversation it turns out to be.

Think of the collection process as a lawn mower. You have to put gas in it, turn it on, and push it. If you do not do each step, it will stop. Think of being awarded your judgment as the purchase of your lawn mower. Finding your debtor's assets, getting a writ issued, taking it to the sheriff's office, and selecting a collection procedure is the same as putting gas in your lawn mower and pushing. You need to tell the sheriff what procedure to implement (e.g., bank levy, wage garnishment, or keeper levy). If you do not select a procedure at the sheriff's office, the process will stop—just like the lawn mower.

To get a writ, some states make you complete an application, while others have you complete the actual writ.

TYPES OF WRITS

The most common type of writ in judgment collection is the *writ of execution*. Sometimes this is called different things in different states.

In Michigan, a writ of execution is called a *request and order to seize property*. If you want to get your debtor's automobile, bank account, paycheck, or valuable personal property in Michigan, you will need to have a request and order to seize property issued.

In Georgia, a writ of execution is called a *writ of fieri facias* (writ of fifa). The fifa, once issued, places a lien against the losing party and any real property he or she owns. You may also use it to levy against personal property.

As mentioned earlier, in many states, a writ of execution is used to get your debtor's wages, personal property, bank accounts, and automobiles. However, a few states distinguish between a writ of execution and a writ of garnishment. In those states, a *writ of garnishment* is used to get your debtor's paycheck and the writ of execution is used to seize your debtor's property, such as bank accounts, personal property, and automobile. To keep matters simple, this book refers to writs in general, and you will fill in whether your state requires a writ of execution or a writ of garnishment.

Many states may require you to have your writ issued to a specific county. Read the form you have to file to determine if it needs to be issued to a specific county. If you find out that it must be issued to a specific county, you should wait until you know the location of a particular asset you want to pursue.

Also, you need to find out if your court will issue more than one writ at a time. If your debtor has assets in multiple counties, you may want to have two or three writs issued at once. If you only implement one collection procedure at a time, your debtor might start hiding assets and make it extremely difficult for you to implement a second collection procedure. Ask the clerk of your court if you can get more than one writ issued to the same county at the same time, and if the answer is no, ask if you can get more than one writ at the same time if they are issued to different counties.

GETTING A WRIT ISSUED

To have a writ issued, do the following.

- Complete the required form from the court that entered your judgment. (Be sure to identify the county the asset is in, if required.)
- File the form in the court that entered your judgment.
- Take your writ to the levying officer in the county where the asset you are going after is located.
- Complete the levying officer's form.
- Pay the levying officer's fee.

(See a sample writ of execution in Appendix C.)

In Idaho, to get a writ issued, you have to get a certified copy of your judgment to submit with an application and affidavit for a writ of execution. You do not have to identify in which county the particular asset is located at the time you are filing for a writ, because writs in Idaho are not county-specific.

However, as mentioned earlier, writs are county-specific in many states. You will need to know which asset you are going after and in which county that asset is located before you have a writ issued. Writs are usually good for several months. For example, in California, a writ is good for six months. You will need to have another writ issued if the six-month period passes and your writ expires.

You should add up all costs incurred and interest earned to date before filing for another writ, so your writ will reflect the current total amount due.

WARNING

Some judgment collectors immediately have a writ issued in the county where the debtor lives. The rationale for doing so is to save time. If and when you locate an asset you want to seize, then you will not have to take the time to run down to the courthouse to have a writ issued.

This practice is really unnecessary. Most courts will issue a writ on the spot. However, if your jurisdiction requires that you submit an application for a writ and return either later that day or on another day to actually pick up the writ, then this approach may be of some use to you.

8

Garnishment

A *garnishment* is a collection procedure in which the levying officer takes assets (usually money) owed to your debtor from the party that owes, to satisfy your judgment. A *writ of garnishment* is an order from the court to the levying officer giving the levying officer permission to garnish your debtor's assets. As mentioned earlier, a writ of execution is used for the same procedures for which other states use a writ of garnishment, so to lessen the chance of confusing you, this book refers to all writs as simply "writs."

Usually, a garnishment is served on the third party who has possession of your debtor's money or owes your debtor money in the future. That third party, such as your debtor's bank or employer, has a certain number of days to respond by filing a *memorandum of garnishee,* also called a *garnishee disclosure.* In some states, if the garnishee fails to respond to the garnishment by completing and returning a memorandum of garnishee or garnishee disclosure, it is up to you, the creditor, to take the next step and sue that third party for failing to abide by the garnishment.

In Arkansas, the courts go after that third party for you. The court in Arkansas will enter judgment against that third party after ten days if that third party fails to respond to the garnishment. In Hawaii, the garnishee is not required to return the garnishee disclosure, but may do so to either declare that your debtor is not an employee or that your debtor is not owed any money by the garnishee.

DIFFERENT TYPES OF GARNISHMENT

Some states also distinguish between a garnishment for non-wages (like a bank account) and a garnishment for wages (like a paycheck), also called a *withholding order.* Other states distinguish between periodic garnishments (like a paycheck) and non-periodic garnishments (like a bank account).

Periodic Garnishment

A *periodic garnishment* is a collection procedure in which a third party is ordered to withhold assets owed to your debtor that will be paid in installments, like wages or rent. Some states do not allow garnishments of periodic payments, like rent, without an assignment order, which is discussed in Chapter 13. (See a sample noticed motion in Appendix C.)

Non-Periodic Garnishment

A *non-periodic garnishment* is a court order directing a third party to turn over to the levying officer assets that are owed to your debtor or owned by your debtor at that time. It is a procedure that does not apply to future assets that the third party may possess or owe to your debtor. Some non-periodic garnishments are also referred to as *levies* in many states, so these procedures are discussed further in Chapter 9.

WAGE GARNISHMENT

The phrase *wage garnishment* is the most commonly used term for this procedure; it is sure to be recognized regardless of which state you are collecting your judgment in, even if your state also calls it something else.

A wage garnishment is a procedure used to get money from your debtor's paycheck. The amount of your debtor's pay that you can reach with this procedure is usually a percentage of your debtor's income. A wage garnishment can be the most reliable way to have your judgment paid, because you will receive a steady flow of payments taken directly from your debtor's paycheck.

In most states, your debtor's wages are withheld and given to the levying officer, who then gives the money to you. You are usually not required to do anything once your debtor's wages are being withheld, unless your debtor files a claim of exemption, which is discussed on page 134.

However, in some states it is different. For example, in Hawaii, you are required to provide your debtor's employer with *duplicate receipts* (two sets) for the money withheld and turned over to you. If you fail to provide these receipts, you can forfeit the money already withheld from your debtor's paycheck. In Maryland, you are required to complete a monthly report and give a copy to your debtor and a copy to the garnishee, but you are not to file it with the court. Check with the levying officer who implements your wage garnishment to see if there is anything further required of you once the wage garnishment starts.

To do a wage garnishment, you obviously must know where your debtor works. If you do not know where your debtor works, you will have to conduct a debtor examination.

CONDUCTING A WAGE GARNISHMENT

To get a wage garnishment, do the following.

- Determine the type of writ you need to start this procedure (writ of execution, writ of garnishment, etc.).
- Complete a form for the writ from the court that entered your judgment.
- File the form with the court clerk in the courthouse that entered your judgment. (If you have domesticated a sister-state judgment, you need to get a writ from the court in which you domesticated your judgment.)
- Take the writ to the levying officer in the county where the employer's payroll is processed.
- Pay the levying officer's fee.

Some states place limits on the amount and duration of wage garnishments. For example, in Wisconsin, wage garnishments can only last up to three months, unless your judgment is against an employee of the state or an employee of your local government, in which case it would last until your judgment is satisfied. In California, your wage garnishment will continue until your judgment is satisfied, regardless of who it is against.

Once your debtor's employer starts to withhold money from your debtor's paycheck, he or she will hold onto it for a designated period of time, usually ten days. During that time, your debtor may file a claim of exemption with the levying officer who served the wage garnishment. Your debtor may claim that he or she cannot afford to have that money withheld and doing so will prevent him or her from providing his or her family with the common necessities of life, like food and shelter. If your debtor files a *claim of exemption,* refer to the section in this book titled "Claim of Exemption and Opposition to Claim of Exemption," found on page 134.

If your debtor does not file a claim of exemption or if the claim is denied, his or her employer will continue to withhold the money out of each paycheck. In some states, your debtor's employer will send that money to the levying officer, who will then turn it over to you. In other states, your debtor's employer will turn the money over to you directly.

Usually, if an employer (called the *garnishee*) receives a subsequent wage garnishment, the subsequent garnishment will not be paid until the wage garnishment that was in place first is paid in full.

Also, if your debtor is someone who would quit his or her job to avoid paying your judgment, this procedure will not work. However, if your debtor has no assets other than his or her paycheck, this approach is worth a try. Again, the allowable amount to be withheld through a wage garnishment is a percentage of your debtor's income. Ask the levying officer what that percentage is in your state.

You will not be able to do a wage garnishment on future salary or vacation and sick leave. The employee must have earned the wages before they are eligible to be garnished, and the wages must be currently owed to your debtor.

Your wage garnishment will probably take effect within a few weeks after service of it on the employer, and in most states, will remain in effect until it is paid in full, the debtor quits his or her job, or a specified termination date in the order is reached.

EMPLOYEE VS. INDEPENDENT CONTRACTOR

For a wage garnishment to be successful, your debtor must be working as an *employee*. A lot of people are not employed—they are actually independent contractors. An *independent contractor* is someone who works for him- or herself and enters into a contract for his or her services with a third party. He or she is not an employee of that third party, and therefore does not receive wages for you to garnish.

To determine whether your debtor is an employee or an independent contractor, answer the following two questions as best you can.

- Does my debtor submit invoices for services? If yes, your debtor is an independent contractor. If no, or if you have no idea, move on to the next question.
- Does my debtor have full control over his or her work, or does his or her boss control what he or she does at work? If your debtor has complete control over his or her work, then he or she is probably an independent contractor and a wage garnishment cannot be done. If your debtor does not have complete control over his work—e.g., he or she has to report to work at the same time everyday and answers to someone—then it is possible that he or she is an employee and wage garnishment is an option for you.

If you are still unclear whether or not your debtor is an employee, try calling the company to see if he or she is listed on the phone/voice mail system. If you are still not able to determine whether or not your debtor is an employee and you do not have any other assets to go after, go ahead and process the wage garnishment.

If you are able to determine your debtor is not an employee and is actually an independent contractor of the company in question, do not waste your time processing a wage garnishment.

Many judgment creditors have difficulties determining whether people engaged in certain types of work are independent contractors or employees. The following breakdown may help clarify matters for you.

Temporary Employees

A *temporary employee,* or temp, is actually an employee of the temp agency. You can do a wage garnishment on a temp, but the paperwork would be served on the temp agency, not the location where your debtor reports to work everyday.

Entrepreneurs

Entrepreneurs who are working for themselves and not contracting out their services to anyone else are not appropriate candidates for a wage garnishment because they are not employed and receiving wages. However, if your debtor has started a company like a corporation or LLC and is actually an employee of that company (for example, he or she is the CEO), then you can do a wage garnishment.

Professionals

Professionals who form business entities—such as corporations, LLCs, or LPs—to conduct business are usually considered employees of the entity they form. For example, if your debtor is a doctor and employed by his or her professional corporation, then you can do a wage garnishment.

HOW WAGE GARNISHMENT WORKS

After the levying officer serves your earnings withholding order (wage garnishment) on your debtor's employer, a lien is created on your debtor's income. His or her employer is then legally obligated to notify your debtor of the order, wait the prescribed number of days, and then turn a percentage of your debtor's income over to you at every pay period.

Earning withholding orders for child support and taxes take priority over all other withholding orders. If you know that your debtor has either or both of these types of withholding orders already in place, then it would be a waste of your time to pursue a wage garnishment.

EXEMPTIONS

Your debtor is entitled to an exemption of part of his or her income for living expenses. There are both state and federal laws that dictate how much of your debtor's income can be exempt. This exemption is not the same as a claim of exemption (see page 134 for more information). Ask the levying officer in your area how much of your debtor's income is exempt.

LEVYING OFFICER

The levying officer you need to go to is in the county where the order (wage garnishment or withholding order) is to be served (where payroll is located), and not where it is to be enforced (if they are different counties). For example, if the company's payroll is processed in county A, but your debtor works in county B, the levying officer you use should be in county A, because that is where the payroll department is located. Hire the levying officer in the county where the paperwork needs to be served, not the county where your debtor actually reports to work.

DISADVANTAGES TO A WAGE GARNISHMENT

There are a few disadvantages to doing a wage garnishment. First, you will end up getting paid in installments, which could drag out for a long time. Second, your debtor may become frustrated and simply file for bankruptcy. However, unless he or she is successful with his or her bankruptcy, the mere filing for a bankruptcy will only serve as a delay.

If your debtor quits his or her job, the wage garnishment stops. You will then have to locate your debtor's new employer. If you cannot find his or her new employer, you can conduct an examination hearing to find out that information.

FEDERAL EMPLOYEES AND MILITARY PERSONNEL

Federal employees are able to have their wages garnished to satisfy civil judgments. Service of the earnings withholding order and the writ must be made on the agent for service for the agency where your debtor works. If there is not a registered agent for service, then serve the head of that agency.

Call the number for the personnel office and ask to whom the papers are directed. Such a person is called an *agent for service of process*. Expect to pay an administrative fee for the processing.

It is also possible to garnish the wages of military personnel. You have to complete a form called an *Involuntary Allotment Application* and submit it with a certified copy of your judgment to the military's Defense Finance and Accounting Service.

For the Army, Air Force, Navy, and Marines:
Defense Finance and Accounting Service
Attention: Code GAG
P.O. Box 998002
Cleveland, OH 44199-8002

For the Coast Guard:
Coast Guard Human Resources
Service & Information Center (LGL)
444 S.E. Quincy Street
Topeka, KS 66683-35911

PREMATURE TERMINATION

You may have to wait a period of days, usually upwards of one hundred days from the date of service of the termination order, before filing another withholding order for the same debtor and the same employer. However, if you can show (by a motion to the court for an order allowing you to get another wage garnishment without having to wait the prescribed number of days) there has been a *material* (significant) change of circumstances with your debtor's finances, you may be able to file for another withholding order before the expiration of that time period.

UNCOOPERATIVE EMPLOYER

If your wage garnishment is served on your debtor's employer and no response is received, it can mean that your debtor no longer works for that employer or that the employer owes your debtor nothing. It can also mean that your debtor's employer is just ignoring the order, which can happen. If the employer fails to honor your earnings withholding order for an employee currently under its employment, in many states that employer can then be held liable to you for the amount that was supposed to be withheld. For example, in Maryland, if the garnishee fails to follow the wage garnishment order, you can ask the court to cite the garnishee for contempt of court. If the garnishee is found to be in contempt, costs can be awarded.

You can write your debtor's employer a letter respectfully requesting that the order be followed. You may also request that the employer notify you if your debtor quits or is terminated. Tell the employer that if sending the withholding order to that specific employer was a mistake, you will gladly withdraw the order. If you still do not receive any response, then you need to decide whether to continue pursuing the wage garnishment with that employer, file a civil action against the employer for failing to honor the wage garnishment order, or simply move on and attempt to find another asset of your debtor's to pursue.

SPOUSE'S WAGES

You may be able to reach your debtor's spouse's wages if you live in a community property state, but you will not be able to do so through a wage garnishment. You will probably have to get a court order by a noticed motion to reach your debtor's community property interest in his or her spouse's wages, because a wage garnishment can only reach your debtor's wages.

A *community property* state is a state that declares that each spouse has a 50% interest in all property acquired during marriage before separation, as well as any property enhanced by community assets. The only community property states are Arizona, California, Idaho, Louisiana, Nevada, New Mexico, Texas, Washington, and Wisconsin.

ADDING COSTS

You can continue to add costs you have incurred while collecting your judgment while a wage garnishment is in place. To do so, you need to file a Memorandum of Costs. Once it has been filed, get a certified copy from the clerk and file it with the levying officer. The levying officer can then add those costs to the amount of your judgment to be taken from your debtor's wages.

EXISTING WAGE GARNISHMENTS

If there is already a wage garnishment in place when your order is served on your debtor's employer, then your order probably will not be paid. If your order is served at the same time another order is served, your debtor's employer must honor the order that was issued from the judgment that was entered first in time. If two orders are served to your debtor's employer that were issued from judgments entered on the same day, then your debtor's employer can chose which to honor and which to reject. Hopefully, your order will not be the one rejected.

TERMINATING A WAGE GARNISHMENT

Regardless of how you are paid, as soon as you receive full payment (*satisfaction*) of your judgment—including principal, pre-judgment costs, post-judgment costs, and post-judgment interest—you must file an *acknowledgment of satisfaction of judgment,* or your state's equivalent, with the court. If your judgment is paid and you currently have a wage garnishment in place, you must notify the levying officer that your judgment has been satisfied so that he or she can terminate the wage withholdings. If any excess funds are turned over to you after your judgment has been satisfied, you must return them immediately to your debtor.

As mentioned earlier, garnishing your debtor's income is a slower method to collect your judgment. However, few debtors will actually quit their job to avoid paying a judgment, so the odds are certainly in your favor that you will eventually be paid through this procedure. Just remember, the principal amount of your judgment is still earning interest while you are receiving payments and each payment that you receive should first be credited to the interest accrued and then to the principal amount of your judgment.

9

Levies

A *levy* is the seizure of property owned by your debtor or owed to your debtor, often in the possession of a third party. As previously mentioned, levies are also referred to as "non-periodic garnishments" in some states and as just "garnishments" in other states, but in most states, they are called "levies." The most common types of levies are bank levies, personal property levies, and auto levies.

BANK LEVY

Whether your debtor is an individual or a business, you can implement a bank levy to collect your judgment. A *bank levy* is a collection procedure used to reach money in your debtor's bank account. Of course, this procedure depends on you knowing your debtor's bank account information.

WARNING

Never contact a bank and pretend to be a merchant in an effort to determine if a bank account is still open and contains money. It is a violation of the Gramm-Leach-Bliley Act, 15 U.S.C. § 6821.

The easiest way to obtain your debtor's bank information is simply to have been given a check at some time by your debtor and have either the check itself or a copy. If you have never received a check from your debtor, but have written him or her a check, you should get a copy of that check, both front and back, from your bank.

When you get the copy of your check back from your bank, look at the front of it to see if there is an inked fingerprint on it. If there is an inked fingerprint on the front of it, then your debtor did not deposit the check into his or her own account. He or she went to your bank and cashed it. Your debtor's account information will not be on the check, so it is of no use to you. If there is not a fingerprint on the check, turn it over to see if the account number is on the back and is legible.

If you can read the account number and the name of the bank on the back of the check, then you are able to proceed with a bank levy. If you are not able to read the information, take the check to your own bank and find someone to help you read it. If you are not successful at your own bank, then try another bank. Keep trying until you can find someone to help you.

Of course, if neither of the scenarios mentioned above have happened to you, you can always conduct a debtor examination to find out where your debtor banks. (see Chapter 4.)

To get a bank levy, do the following.

- Complete the required form to get a writ from the court that entered your judgment.
- Make sure to have the writ issued to the county where the bank is located. Some banks will allow a bank levy to be served to any branch where your debtor opened his or her account, while other banks have a central location to process bank levies. Check with the levying officer to find out about your particular debtor's bank. If the levying officer cannot provide that information to you, call the bank yourself.
- File the form with the court that entered your judgment.
- Take your writ directly to the levying officer.
- Complete the levying officer's form.
- Pay the levying officer's fee.

For example, to get a bank levy in Connecticut, complete a Bank Execution Proceedings Application and Execution form and file it with the court that entered your judgment. Once you are given the execution order, take it to the levying officer.

Once a bank levy is served on an account, the debtor usually wises up and stops using that account. This is not always true, especially for business accounts. It can be costly for a business to move its accounts, so a business may actually continue to use the very account that you just emptied. Consider implementing a second bank levy on the same account if your debtor is a business. However, if your debtor is an individual and your judgment is not fully satisfied, you will probably have to find another account of your debtor's or another asset altogether.

Service

You can have the civil division of the sheriff's department serve your bank levy, or you can hire a process server. There are advantages and disadvantages to both choices. The timing of service of a bank levy can be very important to its success. For example, if you have a business that only deposits into its bank account during the first week of the month, but then clears the account out by the second week, it is essential that your bank levy be served between the first and second weeks of the month. Otherwise, there will not be any money in the account when the bank levy is served.

The same problem can exist with individual debtors. If you hire the sheriff's department to serve your bank levy, you will have to wait until the sheriff's deputy has time to serve it. If you hire a process server, you can tell that person exactly when to arrive. You will have to pay more for a process server, but it can be worth the money. Process servers can charge double that of a sheriff's deputy, but can be worth it if the bank levy is served at the correct time.

You will only be able to use a process server to handle non-possessory levies. A *non-possessory levy* is any process in which the property is not immediately changing possession, such as a wage garnishment or bank levy. A possessory levy, on the other hand, is a process in which possession of the item to be levied on changes possession immediately, such as an automobile levy. Any time you implement a possessory levy, you must use the sheriff's department.

Process Server vs. Registered Process Server

The difference between a process server and a registered process server is as simple as it sounds: a *registered process server* has registered with the county in which he or she does business and a process server has not registered. Many counties are now requiring process servers to register and be bonded to conduct business. There are plenty of process servers who can deliver your paperwork without being registered, but in some counties, you need a registered process server for a bank levy. Check with a court clerk before hiring a process server to serve your paperwork.

Sample Bank Levy

In some states, the process of getting a bank levy involves many additional steps. In Wisconsin, the process is unusually involved.

To get a bank levy in Wisconsin, do the following:

- Complete a Garnishment Summons, Form SC-503, with as much information as you have.
- File the form with the clerk of the court that entered your judgment.
- Serve your debtor a copy.
- Serve the garnishee (the bank) a copy.
- Pay the garnishee a fee.
- The court will set a hearing for you to attend. The garnishee has until that hearing date to file an answer and serve you and the debtor. If the garnishee fails to answer, it may become liable (responsible) to you for the amount of your judgment.
- If the garnishee answers and provides information about your debtor's accounts, you then file a motion for the court to order the garnishee to turn over the money to you.
- Serve your motion to your debtor and the garnishee.

Do not be discouraged by the process in Wisconsin, even if you live in Wisconsin. It can be done. You will just have to jump through a few more hoops when serving bank levies.

Correcting Debtor's Name

It is essential that the name on your judgment be one of the names on the bank account in question. If there is a spelling error in your judgment, then you may need to amend or correct it before initiating a bank levy. In most courts, motioning the court to amend the name on a judgment is fairly easy. You file a request (probably a noticed motion) with the court that entered your judgment. The court will set a hearing and notify the other party, or you will need to serve him or her. You must attend that hearing and explain to the court what type of amendment or correction you are requesting. (Check the code containing civil procedure in your jurisdiction for the exact requirements.)

If your court does not have standardized forms, you will probably have to draft and file a noticed motion to request the court to amend your judgment. Check your state's code of civil procedure or its equivalent and your court's local rules for further instruction. (See the "Noticed Motion" section on page 125 for more information.)

To correct the name on your judgment, do the following.

- Get the required form, or if there is not a required form, draft a motion.
- Complete the form and attach supporting material establishing that your debtor's name is in fact different from what is on the judgment.
- File the form with the court that entered your judgment. If you have domesticated your judgment, then you would file it in that new court.
- If a hearing is required, attend the hearing and bring your evidence.

If the error is a clerical error by the court, you will want to ask the court clerk if there is a standardized form to request the court to correct your judgment. In such a case, you will probably not have to attend a hearing.

PERSONAL PROPERTY LEVY

If your debtor has any personal property that has significant value, you might consider having it seized and sold. You have to know exactly what the property is and where it is located. A *personal property levy* requires either your debtor to turn property over to the levying officer immediately after being served with the levy or the levying officer to take the property from your debtor without your debtor's cooperation.

To get a personal property levy, do the following.

- Complete the required form for a writ, or your state's equivalent.
- File it with the court that entered your judgment.
- Complete a notice of levy form, or your state's equivalent.
- Take your writ and your notice of levy to the levying officer (sheriff's department) in the county where the personal property is located.

In most states, you can implement a personal property levy at the same time you have a lien on your debtor's real property (by recording an abstract of judgment). In Kentucky, however, you are required to execute your judgment on your debtor's personal property before you go after any of his or her real property.

Any of your debtor's personal property that you have seized will be held for a number of days, usually ten. Your debtor may file a claim of exemption concerning that property before the expiration of that time period. If he or she does not file a claim of exemption, the property will then be sold at auction and the money turned over to you.

AUTO LEVY

An *auto levy* is the seizure of an automobile owned by your debtor. The levying officer seizes the automobile and stores it. It is then put up for sale at a public auction. The levying officer will not turn the debtor's car over to you.

Auto levies are rarely profitable, because the seized auto is sold at an auction. It usually sells for far less than what it is worth. However, if you end up buying the auto yourself at the auction, it could be a great opportunity for you to buy a car at a low price and resell it at market price. Ask the levying officer if you can attend the auction and bid on the auto yourself. Whatever you paid for the auto (minus the cost of the auction, and any prior liens on the car) is what would be applied toward satisfying your judgment.

Auto levies are also very expensive. You usually have to pay several hundred dollars to the levying officer in advance to cover the cost of seizing the auto and storing it until the auction. You can recover these costs if the auto sells for enough to cover all of the deductions that must be covered.

Your debtor is entitled to an exemption right off the top of the money recovered from the auction. The amount of the allowable exemption varies from state to state. You can find out what the allowable exemption is in your state by calling the civil division of your local sheriff's office and asking how much the debtor's exemption is for an auto levy. Be sure to ask how much the exemption is for a *personal use vehicle* and also for a *commercial use vehicle,* as the amounts will be different.

If your debtor financed his or her car, the bank must also be paid out of the proceeds. In fact, if the car is financed, the car cannot sell for less than the amount owed to the bank. If a bidder offers more than the bank is owed, the car is sold, the bank is paid, your debtor is paid his or her exemption, costs are taken out, and whatever is left is yours.

As you can see, unless your debtor's auto is very expensive and paid off, it will probably not generate very much money to be applied toward your judgment. An auto levy should only be used as a last resort.

If you do chose to do an auto levy, do the following.

- Complete the required form to get a writ, or your state's equivalent.
- File it with the court that entered your judgment.
- Take your writ, or your state's equivalent, to the sheriff's office in the county where your debtor's car is located. The car must not be in a private garage. If it is, you must get a court order for the levying officer to enter a *private place*.

Buy the Auto Yourself

Find out when the auction is being held and take a friend. If there are no prior liens on the car, all that is required for the auction to take place is competitive bids. Your friend bids the opening price and you bid just a few dollars over that price. If there is not anyone else present, you get the car for a good deal and the debtor gets very little applied to your judgment.

10

Special Procedures

Sometimes you need to take different measures from the more common methods of collecting a judgment. You may be able to get your debtor's driver's license suspended, and if he or she is professional, you may be able to get his or her professional license suspended until he or she pays the debt. These procedures are not available to everyone, but they may apply to your situation.

DRIVER'S LICENSE SUSPENSION

If your judgment resulted from your debtor's operations of a motor vehicle, suspending his or her driver's license until your judgment is satisfied may be an option. Check the laws in your jurisdiction to see if this procedure is available and what additional requirements must be met. Start by contacting the Department of Motor Vehicles in your state. Your judgment usually must be for a certain dollar amount and have been *unsatisfied* (unpaid) for a minimum amount of time.

Also, your judgment usually must have written on it that it resulted from your defendant's operation of a motor vehicle in that state. If your judgment was based on damage from a car accident, but the judgment does not specifically state that it was, then you will need to file a motion to amend it.

To suspend your debtor's driver's license, do the following.

- Wait the time required by your state to get a driver's license suspension.
- Get the form from the court clerk or the department of motor vehicles, or your state's equivalent office (Commissioner of Public Safety in Minnesota) and complete it.
- If it is required that you file the form with the court, do so. If it is required that you send the form directly to the government agency, do so.

In California, there are actually two options for suspending your debtor's driver's license. If your judgment is for $500 or under, you can have your debtor's driver's license suspended if it remains unpaid for a period of ninety days after your judgment becomes final (after any appeal period has passed). This type of suspension will usually last for a specified period of time. If your judgment remains unpaid after that time expires, investigate whether you can apply for another suspension. The second option is for judgments of $500 and more. For such judgments, you only have to wait for thirty days after your judgment becomes final. This type of suspension will last until your judgment is paid. If this is not the case in your state, then investigate whether or not you can apply for another suspension once your first suspension expires.

Debtors tend to take any action from a government agency very seriously. Unless your particular debtor lives without regard for the law or his or her driver's license, suspension of his or her driver's license will usually encourage your debtor to find a way to get you your money.

Debtor Interference

Your debtor may have the suspension lifted if he or she initiates a payment plan through a court order. Such requests are usually granted. However, if such a request is made, you should consider filing an opposition. Also, if your debtor fails to make any of the payments, you can then request the court to set aside the payments and then file for another driver's license suspension.

If you decide to oppose your debtor's request to make payments, do the following.

- If a standardized form is available for your opposition, complete it. If not, draft an opposition on pleading paper.
- Have someone serve your debtor (probably by mail) and complete a proof of service.
- File your opposition and proof of service with the court.
- Pay the fee, if there is one.
- Attend the hearing and argue why your debtor should not be permitted to make payments, such as:
  - Your debtor makes enough money to pay his or her bills and pay your judgment off.
  - Your debtor has misrepresented information on the financial statement he or she submitted with his or her request to make payments.
  - The amount of payment offered by your debtor will not even cover the interest your judgment is accruing annually.

PROFESSIONAL LICENSE SUSPENSION

Judgment debtors who hold professional licenses can be forced to pay civil judgments by the governing boards that issued their licenses. Professional licenses include (but are not limited to) those for attorneys, contractors, and real estate agents/brokers. If your debtor holds a professional license, check to see if you can file to have that license to practice in his or her field suspended until your judgment has been satisfied.

For such a suspension to be granted, the underlying judgment must have been related to your debtor's work in his or her field. Suspending your debtor's license to practice his or her profession is a huge incentive for your debtor to find a way to pay you. However, you may be cutting off his or her only means to pay you. Think carefully before you take action. You may want to write your debtor a letter warning, not threatening, him or her that you plan to suspend his or her professional license on a specified date unless you receive payment in full. If your debtor offers you a payment plan, consider it. It would certainly be better than no money at all. However, if you think your debtor is just jerking you around, proceed with the suspension.

There are many professions that offer assistance to consumers (that was you before you got your judgment, if your judgment is related to your debtor's profession) collecting their judgments against individuals who practice in that profession. For example, real estate agents/brokers and contractors offer such assistance. Whichever professional license your debtor holds, check to see if you can have it suspended. Contact the state board that governs the particular profession and ask for assistance.

Business Debtors

Collecting a judgment against a business can be much easier than collecting a judgment against an individual. Businesses are less likely to disappear than individuals, even if you are hot on the trail of an asset it owns.

Your first step should be to write your business debtor a demand letter. Find out to whom in the company your letter should be addressed and send it to his or her attention. Wait until any appeal period has passed before you send your letter. Respectfully ask that your judgment be paid immediately. Give your debtor two weeks to submit payment. If you do not receive full payment within that time, initiate collection proceedings. There are procedures available to assist you to collect your judgment against a business that are not available when your debtor is an individual. If the business has a cash register and a regular cash flow, you may be able to hire the levying officer to go out to the business and sit there for blocks of time (e.g., eight, twelve, or twenty-four hours) and take all the cash and checks that come into the business. Alternately, you can decide on the less expensive method of hiring the levying officer to go out and make a one-time grab into the cash register and take all the cash.

You can also go after the bank accounts of the business, just like you can with an individual debtor. Do not worry if your debtor is a corporation (Inc.) or a limited liability company (LLC)—you can still collect your judgment the same way you would if your debtor were a sole proprietor or a partnership.

If you do not have any information about the business's assets, you will have to identify a person within the company who knows about the company's assets, which can be difficult to figure out, and call that person in for an examination hearing, which would actually be a third-party examination. You are able to address your examination order to the company and not name an individual, but you leave yourself without a remedy if the company fails to send someone to your hearing. If you name an individual in the company who has knowledge of the company's assets, and that individual has been served and fails to appear, you are then entitled to the same remedies as you are when an individual debtor fails to attend an examination hearing, like a bench letter and a bench warrant.

The procedures that follow will not work for all types of businesses. Some businesses' financial situations are more similar to individuals, such as consultants or home-based businesses. If your debtor is such a business, refer to the procedures previously discussed concerning collecting a judgment against an individual.

NAME CHANGE

If your debtor is a business and it changes its name, you may file an *affidavit of identity* with the clerk when you are filing for a writ or an abstract of judgment. An affidavit of identity tells the court that your debtor is using a different name—an *also known as* (aka). After approval of your request by a judge or a commissioner, the clerk issuing your abstract of judgment or writ will add that name, allowing you to collect your judgment from your debtor using that different name. For more information about affidavits of identity, refer to page 70.

> ### ⚠ WARNING
>
> An affidavit of identity is not a method to add another debtor post-judgment—it is only a method to identify your debtor's aliases.

KEEPER LEVY

If your judgment is against a business that has a cash register, such as a retail store or a restaurant, then consider using a keeper levy. Not all counties offer this service, so verify that it is available before getting a writ issued.

A *keeper levy* is a procedure in which the levying officer, usually a sheriff's deputy, will go to your debtor's business for a designated period of time and take all the cash and checks that come in to the business. You can usually hire a keeper to stay in the business for eight, twelve, or up to twenty-four hours for a specified number of days. You will be charged by the number of hours per day and the number of days. Remember: you can add the cost of a keeper levy to your judgment by filing a Memorandum of Costs.

To get a keeper levy, do the following.

- Get a writ issued from the court that entered your judgment.
- Take the writ to the levying officer in the county where the business is located.
- Instruct the levying officer to do a keeper levy for the length of time you want and to last the number of days you believe are necessary.
- Pay the required fee.

The levying officer will go to the business and remain for the specified period of time, taking whatever cash and checks the business receives. The money will be held for a number of days, usually ten, to give your debtor the opportunity to file a claim of exemption. If no claim of exemption is filed, the money will then be turned over to you. If a claim of exemption is filed, refer to page 134 for what to do next.

Professional Offices

A keeper placed in a professional office, such as a dentist's office, can be a very effective tool. To ensure the full impact of the keeper, send a copy of the sheriff's instruction form concerning the pending keeper to your debtor. You should get results quickly.

TILL TAP

A *till tap* is similar to a keeper levy, except with a till tap the levying officer takes the cash and checks in your debtor's cash register (often called a *till*) and leaves. He or she does not remain on site, as he or she would for a keeper levy. The levying officer just goes to the cash register, empties it, and leaves. The money is held for a period of days to give your debtor an opportunity to file a claim of exemption. Again, if no claim is filed, the money is then turned over to you.

This procedure requires your debtor to have a cash register, hopefully with a lot of money in it. It is not worth your time to do a till tap on a business that makes one or two $10 sales a day. It would only annoy your debtor.

> ## WARNING
> No matter how tempting it is to do something just to annoy your debtor, that is not your goal. It is never appropriate to use the legal system to harass or annoy your debtor. Every process you initiate must be done in an honest effort to collect your judgment. It is never appropriate to misuse the legal system.

To get a till tap, do the following.

- Get a writ, or your state's equivalent, from the court that entered your judgment. Again, in most states, your writ must be issued to the county in which the business is located.
- Take the writ to the levying officer.
- Fill out the levying officer's form.
- Pay the fee. The fee can be upwards of $200. The levying officer will also take his or her fee out of the register if there is enough money in the till to cover your judgment and his or her fee.
- If there is not enough money to take from your debtor's business, the levying officer will take what is there and you can then add the levying officer's fee for the till tap to your judgment by completing a Memorandum of Costs.

The money that is taken from your debtor's cash register will be held by the levying officer for a period of days to give your debtor the opportunity to file a claim of exemption. If no such claim is filed, the money will then be turned over to you. If a claim of exemption is filed and you receive notice, refer to page 137 for more information.

Bankruptcy

A *bankruptcy* is a legal procedure through which people whose debts have gotten to be overwhelming ask the bankruptcy court to discharge those debts and allow them to start over. Bankruptcies are litigated in federal court and are governed by federal law.

Once a business or an individual files for bankruptcy, all creditor actions (including judgment collections) are immediately and automatically stopped. This is called a *stay*. No additional court order is required. If your debtor files for bankruptcy and a stay is issued, do not lose hope. The stay will remain in effect until the court determines the outcome of your debtor's bankruptcy.

Your debtor's bankruptcy must actually be granted and your particular debt discharged for you to lose your judgment. If your debtor's bankruptcy is not granted, or is granted but your judgment is not discharged, then you can go ahead and collect your judgment.

There are different types of bankruptcy filings, such as Chapter 7, Chapter 11, and Chapter 13. Each type of filing has a specific purpose and a different outcome.

CHAPTER 7

Individuals and businesses in Chapter 7 bankruptcies are seeking *liquidation* (selling off assets). Under Chapter 7, the debtor's nonexempt assets are liquidated (sold) by a trustee and the proceeds are distributed to creditors as required by the Bankruptcy Code (federal law). Most Chapter 7 cases are *no asset* cases, meaning no money will be paid to *unsecured creditors* (creditors who lend money without getting any collateral). The debtor's goal in a Chapter 7 bankruptcy is to discharge all of his or her debts.

If your debtor filed and was granted a Chapter 7 bankruptcy, it is probably a waste of your time to proceed with collections, unless you established a lien on real property prior to the bankruptcy. If you did not establish a lien but want to get your money in the bankruptcy case, you can file a creditor's claim with the bankruptcy court in which your debtor's bankruptcy was filed.

CHAPTER 11

Businesses use Chapter 11 bankruptcy for the purpose of reorganization. Businesses file Chapter 11 and not Chapter 7 because Chapter 11 allows them to retain their assets and remain under the same management. If your debtor filed and was granted a Chapter 11 bankruptcy, check to see if your judgment was discharged. If not, proceed with collections.

CHAPTER 13

Individuals or sole proprietors with a moderate level of debt use Chapter 13 bankruptcy. It is intended as an alternative to liquidation. The debtor is allowed to keep his or her property, but his or her debts have been discharged or negotiated.

WHEN YOUR DEBTOR FILES FOR BANKRUPTCY

Once again, as soon as a business or an individual files bankruptcy, all creditor actions against that debtor, including judgment collection, are automatically stayed. No additional court order is required. It is important to halt all collection activity when a stay is in place. If you do not stop, your debtor or the bankruptcy trustee (the person designated to facilitate the bankruptcy) may obtain a court order to enforce the stay. You could then be liable for actual and punitive damages for a willful violation of the stay.

If it appears that your debtor is likely to file bankruptcy, it is a good idea to start your collections by filing and recording an abstract of judgment in each county where your debtor may have any interest in real property. The filing of an abstract will put a lien on any interest in real property that your debtor may own. It is also a good idea to file a personal property judgment lien with the secretary of state.

NON-DISCHARGEABLE DEBTS

There are debts that cannot be discharged in a bankruptcy. If someone incurs a debt for the basic necessities of life (food, clothing, shelter, etc.), he or she cannot later have that debt discharged in a bankruptcy. Also, if your judgment is for one of the following non-dischargeable debts, you can go ahead with collections after the stay is lifted or expires:

- spousal or child support;
- certain nonsupport marital property division obligations;
- debts arising while acting in a fiduciary capacity, such as embezzlement (a type of theft);
- debts arising from the debtor's willful and malicious injury to another person or his or her property;
- debts for money, property, services; or an extension, renewal, or refinancing of credit to the extent obtained by false pretenses or representations; or actual fraud; and,
- debts for death or personal injury caused by the debtor's operation of a motor vehicle while intoxicated from using alcohol, drugs, or another substance.

If your judgment is not for one of the debts mentioned above, but you still want to pursue your money, file a creditor's claim in your debtor's bankruptcy action in federal court. If your debtor listed your debt in his or her bankruptcy case, you will receive notice from the court. To file your creditor's claim, contact the court that is handling the case and find out how to file and when it is due.

Oppositions and Court Orders

Most of the procedures discussed in this chapter might be beyond what you will need to collect your judgment. They are included to make you aware of all of the possibilities available to you to help you collect your judgment.

OPPOSITION TO DEBTOR'S MOTION FOR COURT-ORDERED PAYMENTS

Your debtor may file a motion to the court to allow him or her to make monthly installment payments. You will receive notice if such a request is made. You can oppose this request by writing an *opposition* and filing it with the court. The court will probably not have a standardized form for your opposition, so you will have to draft something on your own. You should also have someone give your debtor a copy of your opposition and file a proof of service with the court. Attend the hearing if one is scheduled and make your opposition orally in court. If your debtor's request is granted, you will have to accept the payments. If your debtor's request is denied, go ahead with collections.

In Illinois, if you oppose the court ordering payments and it orders them anyway, the payments must be enough to pay your judgment off in three years.

If your debtor misses a payment, you can go back to court by filing a motion to set aside the judgment debtor's installment payments, also called an *affidavit of default,* to kick out the payments the court ordered. If you can get the payments set aside, you can collect your judgment in full, just as you would have had the payments never been ordered.

COURT ORDERS

You may need the assistance of the court to help you collect your judgment. To get the court's assistance, you have to file a request in writing, called a *motion.* When you motion a court to do something, you will probably have to file that motion on pleading paper. *Pleading paper* has numbers that run down the left side of the paper. If you have a word processing program on your computer, check to see if you have "pleading paper" as one of your templates. If you do, you will be able to draft your motion and print it straight from your home computer. If you do not, then you can find blank pieces of pleading paper at **www.uslegalforms.com/paper.htm**. Be sure to space your text to match the numbering down the left side of the page.

NOTICED MOTION

A *noticed motion* is a request that is made by filing documents with the court requesting a hearing. Next, serve your debtor or third party with a certain number of days' prior notice to let him or her know of your intent to appear in front of the court and ask for an order. In this context, a court order is a direction to the levying officer or your debtor, instructing one of them to do something, like seize property or turn over property.

Declaration

Along with your motion, you will need to file a declaration detailing the facts of your situation, such as your judgment remains unsatisfied and your debtor has assets that can be used to satisfy your judgment. A declaration is usually formatted in numbered paragraphs. Each paragraph sets out a different fact. At the end of your declaration, you date it, print your name, and sign (usually under penalty of perjury). (See a sample declaration in Appendix C.)

Memorandum of Points and Authorities

You will also need to file a *memorandum of points and authorities,* often called a *memo* or *MPA.* A memo sets out the law on which you are basing your request. For example, if your state has a statute that allows a judgment creditor to have his or her debtor's rights to receive a payment owed by a third party assigned to him or her to satisfy a judgment, then you will reference that statute in your memo. (See a sample memorandum of points and authorities in Appendix C.)

Proposed Order

You will need to draft an order for the court to sign should you win your motion. It is labeled *proposed order* because the court has not yet adopted it as an order.

To file a noticed motion, do the following.

- If your court does not have standardized forms, draft a motion, a declaration, a memorandum of points and authorities, and a proposed order.
- Contact the clerk to determine in which courtroom the motion is to be heard and ask how to schedule a hearing. The clerk will probably tell you which days that courtroom hears such matters, e.g., Tuesdays and Thursdays at 9:00 a.m., and then you choose the day. (Your court may handle all the scheduling.)
- Write the day and time on your motion.
- Have someone serve your debtor a copy of your motion, declaration, memorandum of points and authorities, and proposed order with the minimum number of days before the hearing as is required by your court. The number of days required for a noticed motion will be significantly more than the number of days required for an ex parte motion.
- Have a proof of service completed by whoever serves your documents.
- File the original of your motion, declaration, memorandum of points and authorities, and the proof of service with the clerk in the filing room of the court that entered your judgment.
- You will be charged a fee, so go to the courthouse prepared to pay it.
- If your court has a tentative ruling line (see page 128), call it the night before to see if you need to go to court to argue your motion.

EX PARTE MOTION

An *ex parte motion* is a request made by filing the same documents as for a noticed motion, but requesting a hearing and serving the other party only a short period of time before your scheduled hearing date. Check the applicable rules in your state to determine how much notice is required for an ex parte motion. *Ex parte* means without the other party, which does not mean the other party will not attend or is not allowed to attend. It just means, in this context, with less notice than a noticed motion. Make sure you determine before you begin whether your jurisdiction requires motions for whatever you are seeking to be noticed or if they can be made ex parte.

To file an ex parte motion, do the following.

- If your court does not have standardized forms, draft a motion, a declaration, a memorandum of points and authorities, and a proposed order.
- Contact the clerk to determine in which courtroom the motion is to be heard and ask how to schedule a hearing. The clerk will probably tell you which days that courtroom hears such matters, e.g., Tuesdays and Thursdays at 9:00 a.m., and then you choose the day.
- Write the day and time on your motion.
- Have someone serve it on your debtor with the minimum number of days before the hearing as is required by your court (which will be considerably less than that required for a noticed motion). You may even be able to notify your debtor by phone or fax.
- Have a proof of service completed by the person who serves your documents.
- File the original of your motion, declaration, memorandum of points and authorities, proposed order, and the proof of service with the clerk in the filing room that entered your judgment.
- You will be charged a fee, so go to the courthouse prepared to pay it.
- If your court has a tentative ruling line, call it the night before to see if you need to go to court to argue your motion.

If you fail to apply for the order correctly, you will not only waste your time and money, you will most likely be reprimanded by the commissioner or judge whose time you also will have wasted. If you are required to apply by noticed motion, you will need to determine how your motion must be served on your judgment debtor or third party (and probably also your debtor)—whether it must be personally served or may be served by the mail. Make sure you understand the process before jumping in.

TENTATIVE RULINGS

Some courts have a *tentative ruling line* that you need to call the night before the hearing on your motion is scheduled. A tentative ruling line is usually an automated phone line that will give you the court's tentative ruling on your motion—the way the court is leaning on its decision based on the papers submitted (your motion and the other party's opposition, if one was filed). If the tentative ruling is in your favor, you probably do not have to do anything. If you do not hear from the other party that night, you probably do not have to go to the hearing and the court will enter its tentative ruling as its final decision. If the tentative ruling is against you, you probably need to contact the other party by phone (or your state may allow you to contact by fax or email) and notify him or her that you intend to go to the hearing and argue your motion. You must give the other party notice of your intent to attend the hearing, or the court will probably not allow you to argue. Also, draft a proof of service that you notified the other party and bring that proof of service to the hearing.

ASSIGNMENT ORDERS

If your debtor receives, or will receive in the future, a stream of payments from almost any source, you can probably get an order from the court to have your debtor *assign* (give to you) his or her right to receive that payment. You can reach property through an assignment order that would

not otherwise be subject to execution, such as property located out
your state. Otherwise, to reach property located outside of your state
would have to first domesticate your judgment in that new state.

Stream of Payments

A *stream of payments* is a pattern of payments to your debtor that is
predictable. If your debtor gets regular payments from a third party
(excluding family support payments such as child support), you can get
those payments through an assignment order. Why wouldn't you just have
the debtor served with a notice of levy by the levying officer? A notice of
levy must be served at exactly the time of distribution of the money, which
can be very difficult. It is also only a one-time event. An assignment order
gives you the right to receive the money whenever it is disbursed and
continues until either your judgment is satisfied or the payments in question are completed.

Streams of payment include:
- rents;
- royalties;
- payments from patents, copyrights, or trademarks;
- commissions; and,
- accounts receivable.

To get an assignment order, do the following.
- File a noticed motion with the court that entered your judgment.
- Have someone serve your debtor with the required notice that you will
  be asking the court to order him or her to assign his or her right to
  receive payments to you.
- File a proof of service with the court.

- Attend the hearing and explain to the court why you are entitled to receive the payments otherwise due to your debtor.
- Once the order is signed by the court, have it served to the third party that owes the money to your debtor.

TURNOVER ORDER

You may run into a situation where the only assets your debtor has are kept in his or her home or garage, or on his or her person, like a home computer or a valuable watch. To reach such an item stored in a *private place,* you will have to get a court order to either have your debtor turn the property over to the levying officer or have the levying officer seize it and sell it. If the property you are after is located in a private place and you want your debtor to turn it over to the levying officer, you will need a turnover order.

A *turnover order* is an order from the court that is used to reach property your debtor is keeping in a private place or out of your state. If you are aware of a particular asset worth a significant amount of money that your debtor keeps in his or her house or office, on his or her person, or in another state, you can get a turnover order from the court ordering your debtor to turn that item over to a levying officer to be sold.

The first step to getting a turnover order is to have a writ issued to the county where the property that you are after is located. This requirement might vary from jurisdiction to jurisdiction. If your jurisdiction requires a writ to be issued prior to obtaining the order, get the writ prior to filing for your hearing and indicate in your motion that a writ has already been issued. Check with your court's local rules to determine if your motion needs to be made by a noticed motion or whether it can be made ex parte.

You may also use a turnover order during your debtor examination to get your debtor to turn over to you any and all cash or valuable jewelry he or she has with him or her. For example, if you notice your debtor has on what you believe is expensive jewelry, pull out your turnover order, fill in the blanks with the description and location of the jewelry, and ask the clerk to have the judge or commissioner sign it. Not many judges like to sign these types of orders. Be prepared for the judge to come out and say something like, "Can't we find a way to get this judgment paid without having to take this man's watch?" Your response should be, "Your Honor, my debtor is either unresponsive or evasive to my questions and I have no other choice but to turn to the assets that he carries on his person." This should be enough to get the judge to help you get some information out of your debtor.

When drafting your motion, regardless of whether it is a noticed motion or an ex parte motion, you will probably need to include the following:

- motion for turnover order;
- memorandum of points and authorities in support of your motion;
- declaration (from you) in support of motion for turnover order; and,
- proposed order.

It is possible that you may consolidate the motion, memorandum, and declaration into one document.

SEIZURE ORDER

If the property you are after is located in a private place and you want the levying officer to seize the property and sell it at auction instead of having your debtor turn it over, you will need a court order for the levying officer to go in and get it, called a seizure order. If the property was not in a private place, you could just use a notice of levy.

A *seizure order* is required if the asset that you want the levying officer to seize is in a private place, like a home or a garage. A seizure order is similar to a turnover order and is obtained in the same way. A seizure order is directed to the levying officer, ordering him or her to take the property located in a private place. For example, you would not use a seizure order to get the watch your debtor is wearing, but you would use a seizure order to get the expensive computer in his or her home. As a general rule, use a turnover order to reach an asset that your debtor carries on his or her person and a seizure order to reach an asset that your debtor stores in his or her house, garage, or car.

To get a seizure order, you will need to file a noticed motion (some states may allow you to get a seizure order ex parte) and serve your debtor with the required number of days prior to the hearing.

CHARGING ORDER

If your debtor is a partner in a business partnership, you cannot use a wage garnishment to get his or her salary, because partners in partnerships are not given salaries; they are given *draws*. To reach a partner's draw, you need a court order, called a charging order. A *charging order* orders the partnership to pay you a percentage of the money normally owed to your debtor as a partner draw.

To get a charging order, you will probably need to file a noticed motion and serve your debtor the required number of days prior to the hearing. Follow the instructions to file a noticed motion found on page 126, but title the order "Judgment Creditor's Noticed Motion for Charging Order."

MOTION TO VACATE

A *motion to vacate* is a request to the court by your debtor to kick out your judgment, something you do not want to have happen. The grounds for a successful motion to vacate will vary from state to state. You will probably only encounter a motion to vacate in two situations:

1. Your debtor was never served (or claims to have never been served) in the underlying case and did not attend the hearing—he or she learned about your judgment when you first started a collection procedure, like a bank levy. OR
2. Your judgment has been domesticated to a new state and your debtor is now challenging the interest or costs added to your judgment during the domestication process.

An *opposition* is your statement to the court explaining why you oppose the court vacating your judgment and on what legal grounds you base your opposition. Your basic argument is that your debtor was served properly and simply chose not to come to court. If his or her motion to vacate is based on an error in calculation with the interest or costs, state that he or she is simply mistaken. Hopefully, your debtor will never file a motion to vacate and you will not have to deal with this section at all. However, if he or she does file a motion to vacate, follow the steps discussed very carefully.

If a motion to vacate is filed, a hearing will be scheduled and you will be given notice of the date and time. Then do the following.

- Draft an opposition, addressing each point your debtor raised in his or her motion to vacate your judgment.
- Have someone serve your debtor a copy and complete a proof of service.

- File your opposition with the court, along with the proof of service.
- Attend the court hearing and argue that your defendant was served properly or that the interest or costs were calculated correctly and that the court should deny your debtor's motion to vacate.

If the situation described in number two occurs, the court would probably not kick out your entire judgment and leave you with no judgment at all simply on a miscalculation of interest. The old judgment would be vacated and a new judgment with the correct interest would be entered.

If your debtor files a motion to vacate, another stay will probably be ordered until his or her motion is heard. If you are confused about how to handle a motion to vacate, check with a practice guide on "civil procedure after trial" for assistance.

CLAIM OF EXEMPTION AND OPPOSITION TO CLAIM OF EXEMPTION

Once you have levied on, garnished, or seized some of your debtor's money or property, he or she may put up a fight to get it back. Your debtor would file a *claim of exemption* with the levying officer who took his or her money or property. Your debtor will argue that the money or property taken is exempt for reasons allowable under local or federal law. He or she will have to file a financial statement with this claim, so be sure you get a look at it. If your debtor files a claim of exemption, he or she will have to do so within a very short period of time after the collection procedure you implemented was put into place. You will receive notice of your debtor's claim of exemption from the levying officer. You can file an opposition with the court that entered your judgment. Act quickly! You will only have a few days to respond by filing an opposition.

> # WARNING
> An asset is not exempt unless it is found to be exempt by the court. Let the courts determine if a particular asset is exempt. File an opposition to your debtor's claim. Put up a fight!

In an *opposition,* you oppose your debtor getting to keep his or her money or property. It is also called a *motion to contest claim of exemption* in some states. If you do not file an opposition, it is likely that your debtor will get the money or property released. It is important that you put up a fight. If you do not, then every time you attempt to get your money, your debtor will know that all he or she has to do is file a claim of exemption. Make your debtor prove to the court that the money in question is either from a protected source, like disability or child support, or is needed for his or her necessities of life, like food, shelter, or clothing. You will usually have a set number of days, such as ten days in California or five days in Idaho, to file your opposition to claim of exemption.

For example, to file an opposition in California, you would do the following.

- Complete the required forms from the court that entered your judgment.
- File the original notice of opposition to claim of exemption with the levying officer and a copy of it with the court.
- File the original of the notice of hearing for an order determining the claim of exemption with the court that entered your judgment.
- File a copy of it with the levying officer. The court will schedule a hearing to determine the validity of your debtor's claim of exemption.
- Serve your debtor with your opposition.
- File a proof of service with the court.

Attend your hearing and make the best argument you can for why the court should deny your debtor's claim of exemption.

Your state may have a simplified version of this process. Make sure you determine what your state requires before you get started.

The following are acceptable reasons to deny a debtor's claim of exemption.

- Your debtor's income is sufficient to pay for his or her *common necessities of life* and to pay your judgment or make payments toward your judgment. Support your argument by referring to your debtor's financial statement, which was attached to his or her claim of exemption.
- Your debtor was misleading or dishonest on the financial statement he or she filed with his or her claim of exemption.
- The basis that was given to support your debtor's claim of exemption is not one recognized by law.

There are many other reasons you can offer to the court to deny your debtor's claim of exemption. Concentrate on the facts of your debtor's financial statement. Do not just say that your debtor is liable and that you have a judgment. The court already knows that you have a judgment. You have to state specifics or the court will grant your debtor's claim of exemption and you will lose that money.

Necessities of Life

Your debtor may claim an exemption of all or part of his or her income because he or she needs it to support him- or herself and a family. That exemption may be granted if he or she is able to make a good argument. However, this exemption is not typically available if the underlying debt that your judgment was based on was also for the common necessities of life, like rent or food. Check your state's code of civil procedure for verification that this type of law exists and applies to your judgments.

Timing

If you start a collection procedure, like a wage garnishment, a claim of exemption can usually be filed any time during the withholding period. However, a claim of exemption must be filed within a certain number of days during a bank levy or an auto levy. Check your state's code of civil procedure for the exact time limits.

Notice

As previously mentioned, if your debtor files a claim of exemption, you will be notified by the levying officer, usually by mail. In addition to the claim of exemption paperwork, you should also receive directions on how to file an opposition.

It is recommended that you attach and file a copy of your debtor's claim of exemption and financial statement with the court at the time you file your opposition.

TIMING OF COLLECTION PROCEDURES

Timing can be the key to your success in many of the collection procedures discussed in this book. For example, many people have money in their bank accounts on payday and for a few days afterwards. Once they have paid their bills, their bank accounts dwindle down to spending money until their next payday. Sound familiar? Keeping this in mind, it would benefit you to have your bank levy served on your debtor's bank the day after payday. For your business debtors, the best time to have a bank levy served is the day before the business pays its employees or accounts payable. For a landlord, try the day or two after he or she receives the rent from his or her tenants. Think before you act.

Escrow Accounts

If you are attempting to seize money in an escrow account, when you should garnish the escrow account is determined by whether your debtor is the seller or buyer.

If your debtor is the seller, he or she does not have any interest in the buyer's money until the conditions of escrow have been satisfied. Therefore, your garnishment of the escrow account must be served at the close of escrow, but before disbursement of the money.

If your debtor is the buyer, the money belongs to your debtor before and up until escrow closes. Therefore, your garnishment of the escrow account must be served prior to the closing of escrow.

Controlling Time

You can never totally control the timing of a collection procedure. You can, however, influence it greatly by hiring a process server and instructing him or her when to start the procedure. When you hire the sheriff's department to carry out a collection procedure, you are at the mercy of its schedule and availability. When you hire a process server instead of using the sheriff's department, you are paying to have that individual start the procedure at exactly the time when you need it to be done. The sheriff's department is a reliable and effective presence when implementing some collection procedures, but process servers get the job done when timing is critical.

STEP 4

YOUR ACTION PLAN

14

Make a Plan

Now that you have found at least one of your debtor's assets, it is time to make a plan to turn that asset into cash. If you only found one asset, then your plan is pretty straightforward. If you found several assets, you will need to put them in some kind of order of importance.

The first thing you will always do, regardless of what assets you have found, is file an *abstract of judgment,* or your state's equivalent. Once you have filed an abstract (or multiple abstracts) with the court, record an original in every county in which you suspect your debtor has any interest in real property.

PRIORITIZE THE ASSETS

Next, you need to decide in what order you will go after your debtor's assets. The following approach is a suggested order for your action plan.

- File an original abstract of judgment in any county in which you suspect your debtor may own or have any interest in real property.
- Next, go after an asset that can be disposed of easily, like bank accounts.
- Out of that group of assets, go after the asset that is most likely to produce the most money.

ONE WRIT PER COUNTY AT A TIME

In most states, it is possible to have more than one collection procedure going at a time, but you are usually not allowed to have more than one procedure going in the same county at the same time. The court will usually only issue one writ per county at a time. For example, if you have a writ of execution issued to County A for a bank levy and you want to also get a wage garnishment in that same county, you would have to wait until the bank levy is completed. However, if your debtor works in County B, you can have another writ issued to that county. You would have two procedures in play at the same time, but the writs would be issued to two different counties. You can also probably have a writ and an abstract of judgment issued to the same county at the same time, which is why you are encouraged to file an abstract of judgment first, then figure out which asset you are going to go after next.

PROPERTY THAT IS EASY TO HIDE

Some assets are very easy to hide. Property such as bank accounts (saving, checking, etc.), cash, and valuable personal property (jewelry, computers, antiques) can be moved, sold, or relocated. It is therefore critical that you pursue these types of assets first.

Implement a bank levy if you have enough information about your debtor's bank account(s). Next, pursue any valuable personal property. If that property is located in a private place, see the sections on turnover orders and seizure orders on pages 130 and 131.

If your debtor is a business, implement a till tap or keeper levy immediately after implementing a bank levy. If you do not have enough information to do a bank levy, proceed immediately and do a till tap or a keeper levy.

You need to go after these assets quickly. If your debtor figures out what is going on or talks to anyone who understands judgment collection, you can bet he or she will run down to the bank and close his or her account in a matter of minutes. If your debtor has very little money in his or her account, he or she could take it out from the nearest ATM.

LUMP SUM

Next, go after the asset that is likely to get you the most cash. For example, if your debtor is owed a large sum of money in a lump sum from a third party, go after that. A situation like this is not very common in judgment collection because you have to really know your debtor well to have access to this information.

PAYCHECK

Your debtor's paycheck is the most dependable of all the assets you will run across. It is unlikely that your debtor will quit his or her job to avoid paying your judgment. So, whenever you are ready to go after his or her paycheck, after you have tried the assets mentioned above, the paycheck will be sitting there waiting for you.

SAMPLE PLAN

Use this sample situation and the forms found on pages 145–146 to practice what you have learned about collecting a judgment.

During your debtor examination hearing, you found out the following information:

- The debtor is a bus driver for the city. (PAYCHECK)
- He has a bank account at John's Savings and Loan on Smith Street. (BANK ACCOUNT)
- He said he does not own a house in town, but he does own a house up at the lake. (LIEN ON REAL PROPERTY)

Start your analysis by asking, "Which of these assets is the easiest for my debtor to move?" If you answered, "His bank account," you are correct. A bank account can be closed in a matter of minutes. As mentioned earlier, it is unlikely that your debtor would quit his job or sell his lake house to avoid your judgment, so none of those assets are likely to be moved. Consequently, the bank account should be first on your list, right? No! File an abstract of judgment *first!* If you file an abstract of judgment, even if your debtor files bankruptcy and is granted a discharge of his debts in a bankruptcy, your judgment is secured to his property, if he had any before the bankruptcy was granted (like the house at the lake).

Action Tracker

Asset _____

Location _____

Estimated value _____

Detail: _____

_____

_____

Action taken:

Bank Levy _____ Form filed: _____

Wage Garnishment _____ Form filed: _____

Seizure of Personal Property _____ Form filed: _____

Asset _____

Location _____

Estimated value _____

Detail: _____

_____

_____

Action taken:

Bank Levy _____ Form filed: _____

Wage Garnishment _____ Form filed: _____

Seizure of Personal Property _____ Form filed: _____

Accounting Chart

Judgment	Pre-J Costs	Pre-J Interest	Post-J Costs	Post-J Interest	Payments

STEP 5

CASE CLOSED

Closing Your Case

As soon as you collect any money, you should immediately note that in your accounting chart. Remember to apply payments to the interest category first, then to the principle.

It is possible that you will not be able to collect all of the money that you are owed. If you find yourself in this position, you can always take a break and let the balance of your judgment accrue interest. Remember to keep an eye on your statute of limitations. Unless your judgment is exempt from a statute of limitations (such as a judgment for family support in California), your judgment will eventually expire. You must renew it before that time arrives. Also, keep your address updated with the court just in case your debtor decides to pay the court directly. The court will try to reach you at your old address, but it will not hunt you down. If you do not claim it within a certain number of years, your money will be gone. In California, for example, money that is not claimed eventually goes to the state. Do not let this happen to your money.

ACKNOWLEDGMENT OF SATISFACTION OF JUDGMENT

Once your judgment has been fully satisfied, you must acknowledge as much to the court that entered it. The form you file is called an *acknowledgment of satisfaction of judgment,* or *order of satisfaction,* or just *satisfaction of judgment.* Usually, you can complete a simple form and file it. If you fail to acknowledge that your judgment has been satisfied, you may become liable to your debtor for any damages that result.

To file an acknowledgment of satisfaction of judgment, or your state's equivalent, do the following.

- Get the standardized form (if available) from the clerk in the courthouse that entered your judgment.
- Complete the form as best you can.
- Make two copies (both sides).
- File copies and the original with the clerk in the courthouse that entered your judgment.
- Send one of the copies to your debtor.
- Keep one copy for your own records.

In Idaho, you must sign your acknowledgment of satisfaction in front of a notary public. Check the requirements in your state with the court clerk. If you need to sign in front of a notary public, you can usually find one in a copy shop, city hall, or courthouse. You can also look up notaries in the phone book or on the Internet.

Most states require that you acknowledge to the court that entered your judgment within a specified number of days of having your judgment satisfied. For example, in California, you must do so within two weeks, and in Maryland it is within fifteen days. There really is not any reason not to, so do it quickly. It is also recommended that you send your debtor a filed copy.

As you have seen, there are many ways to get your money. The particular way you get it will dictate whether or not you will have to file anything with the court to close out your case.

Judgment Paid to the Court by Bank Check or Money Order

If your judgment is paid in full—including principal, costs (added by a Memorandum of Costs), and interest (added by a Memorandum of Costs)—by check directly to the court instead of you, the court will notify you and then enter your judgment satisfied immediately. You will probably not have to file an acknowledgment of satisfaction with the court, but you will probably have to go to the court and complete a form to have the court cut you a check.

Judgment Paid to You by Bank Check or Money Order

If your debtor gives you a bank check or a money order for the full amount, you should treat it just like cash. You need to file an acknowledgment of satisfaction immediately after you receive it.

Judgment Paid to the Court by Personal Check

If your debtor pays the full amount of your judgment by personal check to the court, the court will not enter a satisfaction of your judgment until the check has cleared the bank. You can count on the process taking several

will probably not have to file an acknowledgment of satisfac-
he court, but you will probably have to go to the court and
complete a form to have the court cut you a check.

Judgment Paid to You by Personal Check

Similarly, if your debtor gives you a personal check, you probably do not
have to file an acknowledgment of satisfaction of judgment until the check
clears. However, you do need to file an acknowledgment of satisfaction as
soon as the check clears. If you deposit the check into your account, your
debtor can still stop payment on the check and your bank will pull the
money right back out of your account, so you may consider taking your
debtor's check directly to your debtor's bank and cashing it.

Writ Returned Satisfied in Full

If your money was recovered through a writ, the writ will be returned to
the court by the levying officer. The writ itself will reflect how much of
your judgment was satisfied. If the writ has been fully satisfied, the court
clerk may enter satisfaction. You should check the procedures of your
court to verify whether or not you need to file an acknowledgment of satisfaction of judgment if a writ is returned satisfied. When in doubt, file an
acknowledgment of satisfaction.

Agreement Reached with Debtor

Your judgment belongs to you and it can be satisfied by a separate agreement
between you and your debtor. You are free to negotiate the satisfaction of your
judgment in any way you would like—within legal bounds, of course. For
example, if your debtor agrees to mow your lawn every week for the entire
summer to satisfy a $2,000 judgment, then both parties are free to enter that
agreement. Once the lawn mowing is complete, you must file an acknowledgment of satisfaction to the court that your judgment has been satisfied.

Judgment Satisfied through Installments

If your judgment was paid in installments, you do not have to file an acknowledgment of satisfaction until your judgment is paid in full. It is your responsibility to keep track of all payments received, interest accrued, and costs incurred. You must notify your debtor when your judgment is satisfied in full and file an acknowledgment of satisfaction with the court.

REMOVING REAL PROPERTY LIENS

If you filed an abstract of judgment, placing a lien on real property or personal property, you must send your debtor notice that satisfaction of your judgment has been acknowledged and that there is a lien that needs to be removed. The notice needs to state in which county an abstract of judgment was filed. Also, note on the notice if you filed an abstract with the secretary of state's office. You do not usually have to file an acknowledgment of satisfaction with the recorder's office or with the secretary of state's office, but you do have to notify your debtor to do so.

DEBTOR'S REQUEST TO ENTER SATISFACTION

Your debtor may file a request directly with the court to enter satisfaction of your judgment. If your debtor is able to provide sufficient proof to the court that your judgment has been satisfied, the court will enter your judgment satisfied.

NEGATIVE MARK ON DEBTOR'S CREDIT REPORT

The three major credit bureaus record civil judgments from the court's files. You have nothing to do with removing any such mark on your debtor's credit report. You did not place it there and it is not your responsibility to remove it. Once you file an acknowledgment of satisfaction, your case is over and your job is done. If your debtor contacts you and requests that you remove your judgment from his or her credit report, tell him or her that he or she needs to contact the credit bureaus and provide each of them with a certified copy of your acknowledgment of satisfaction. This is the debtor's job, not yours.

The three major credit bureaus can be contacted in the following ways.

Experian
888-397-3742
www.experian.com

Equifax
800-685-1111
www.equifax.com

Transunion
877-322-8228
www.transunion.com

Conclusion

As you have seen, each state has its own system of judgment collection. There are many similarities among the fifty states, such as the use of similar terms and processes. These similarities allow you to maneuver your way through your own state's system by learning the big picture of the judgment collection process. As long as you understand the big picture, you can change the names of the procedures and you will still understand how to proceed.

The goal of this book has been to provide you with a user-friendly method to collect your own judgment. Individuals should be able to navigate their way through the courts without having to hire someone else to guide them.

I hope that you have enjoyed this book and have found it helpful in learning the judgment collection process.

Glossary

A

abstract of judgment. A document issued by the clerk of the court in which your judgment was entered. It is then filed with the county recorder's office in each county in which the judgment debtor owns real property. It can also be used to place a lien on a lawsuit the judgment debtor has against someone else.

accounts receivable. Accounts with balances owed by debtors.

acknowledgment of satisfaction. A form the judgment creditor must file with the clerk of court in which the judgment was entered, acknowledging full or partial payment of the judgment.

asset. Anything owned that has monetary value. An asset can be either real property or personal property.

assignee. The recipient of an assignment.

assignment. To transfer one's interest in property, contract, or other rights to another.

assignment agreement. The agreement between assignor and assignee dictating the terms of the agreement.

assignor. The one who assigns his or her interest to the assignee.

appeal. A resort to a higher court for the purpose of obtaining a review of a lower court decision and a reversal or different judgment from that of the lower court.

B
bank levy. Enforcement of a judgment against a judgment debtor's bank account.

bench warrant. An order of arrest issued by a court of law when a party does not appear when ordered to do so. Also called a *body attachment.*

C
caption. The heading on pleadings and legal documents that states the party's name and the party that is submitting the papers.

case number. The number assigned by the court to a lawsuit. Also called a *suit number.*

certified copy. A copy of a document that a court clerk certifies, attesting that the document is an authentic copy. It may be referred to as *exemplified copy.*

claim of exemption. An attempt by a judgment debtor or third party whose assets have been attached, levied against, or seized in an effort to enforce a judgment to have his or her property deemed by a court of law to be exempt and therefore unable to be taken.

co-debtor. A party to a debt. When there is more than one party owing on a debt, the multiple debtors are known as co-debtors.

co-defendant. One of multiple defendants. When there is more than one defendant, the defendants are known as co-defendants.

commissioner. A judicial bench officer, employed by the court to hear cases.

community property. All property acquired during marriage and before separation and any property enhanced with community assets.

contempt. Willful disobedience of a lawful order or willful obstruction of a legislative body in the course of exercising its powers.

continuance. The continuance of the court proceedings in a case to a future date.

corporation. A company structure that is an association of shareholders created under law and regarded as an artificial person by the courts. It has a legal entity entirely separate and distinct from the individuals that operate it.

costs. The money spent in litigation or enforcement of a judgment that is returned to the successful party for the expenses of litigation; more commonly used here to add expenses in judgment enforcement.

D

damages. Monetary compensation that the law awards to one who has been injured by the action of another.

defendant. The party responding to the complaint; the one being sued.

disposable income. The amount of income left over after legally required deductions are subtracted.

docket (n). The list of cases on the court's calendars.

docket (v). To place a judgment on the court's records.

domestication. The process of turning a sister-state judgment into a judgment of a new state.

E

enforce. To cause to take effect or to be fulfilled.

escrow. A holding place or account where property or title to property and the money for the purchase of that property are held until all contingencies on the sale are met and the property and money are distributed to the buyer and seller, respectively.

execution. The seizure of property of the judgment debtor.

exemplified copy. See *certified copy.*

F

fictitious business name. A made-up name used for a business that is either more or less than the owner's legal name, e.g. Bob's Burgers.

foreign judgment. A judgment entered in another state.

fraudulent conveyance. Transference of property without receipt of fair and equal value.

G

garnishee. A third party in possession of property owned or owed to a judgment debtor.

garnishment. An enforcement procedure whereby property owned by the judgment debtor is in the possession of a third party and is ordered to be handed over to the levying officer to satisfy a judgment.

I

installment payments. Payments made on a debt according to a prearranged schedule.

J

judgment. Court order determining the outcome of a case.

judgment creditor. Winning party that is owed by the judgment debtor on a judgment.

judgment debtor. Losing party that owes the judgment creditor on a judgment.

judgment proof debtor. One from whom nothing can be recovered because he or she had no property, his or property is not within the jurisdiction where the judgment was entered, or he or she is protected from execution of the judgment by statute.

K

keeper. A levying officer that goes to a business and takes all the cash and checks that are paid to that business for a specified number of hours and days to satisfy a judgment.

L

lien. An encumbrance to property creating an interest in that property.

limited liability company. A company structure that is a hybrid of a limited partnership and a corporation.

liquidation. A process of determining liabilities and selling assets to apply toward indebtedness.

M

motion. An application to the court requesting an order in favor of the applicant.

N

necessities of life. The basic requirements to survive, including housing, food, and transportation.

non-periodic garnishment. A garnishment used to garnish money that another party holds for the judgment debtor. Once a non-periodic garnishment is served, the money is seized, and the garnishment is over. If there is not enough to satisfy the judgment, another garnishment must be implemented.

non-wage garnishment. A garnishment of property other than the debtor's wages; e.g., a bank account.

notary public. A public officer under civil and commercial law authorized to administer oaths, and to attest to and certify certain types of documents. The seal of a notary public authenticates a document.

notice of appeal. Notice filed by a party to a civil action to initiate an appeal to review an order or judgment.

notice of motion to vacate judgment. A request made and notice given by a party to a case to vacate or cancel a judgment.

O

opposition. A reply filed to oppose another party's request.

order. A decision by a court of law.

P

perfected. All requirements satisfied.

periodic garnishment. A garnishment used to garnish debts that are paid to the judgment debtor on a periodic basis; e.g., rent payments.

personal service. Delivery of the court documents to the actual party.

plaintiff. The one who initially brings a lawsuit.

purchase money. Money to be paid for the purchase of property.

pro tem judge. A judge who substitutes in to oversee a legal proceeding.

process server. Individual that delivers court documents, also known as affecting service of process.

R

registered process server. A process server who has registered with the county in which he or she does business.

request to correct or vacate judgment. A request to a court to correct an error in a judgment, or in the alternative, to vacate or cancel that judgment.

response. The act of responding to a request before the court.

S

service of process. The communication of the process or court papers to the defendant, either by actual delivery or by other methods, whereby the defendant is furnished with reasonable notice of the proceedings against him or her.

security interest. Some right or interest in a claim or piece of property.

sister-state judgment. A judgment entered by another state.

statute of limitations. Any law that fixes the time within which parties must take judicial action to enforce rights or else be thereafter barred from enforcing them.

stay. A judicial order whereby some action is forbidden or held in abeyance until some event occurs or the court lifts the order.

summons. A document that is completed by the plaintiff and issued by the court to the defendant notifying him or her that he or she is being sued.

T

transmutation. The transference of a nonexempt asset into an exempt asset.

V

venue. Place of trial; refers to the possible or proper place or places for the trial of a lawsuit.

W

wage garnishment. A procedure used to enforce a judgment wherein a percentage of the debtor's nonexempt wages are withheld and turned over to the creditor.

writ of execution. An order from the court that entered a judgment to a levying officer to execute a judgment in the specified amount.

Appendix A:
Sample Cases

The two sample cases that follow are hypothetical. Any resemblance to anyone living or dead is completely coincidental. These sample cases walk you through some typical judgment collection situations. You can use them to apply the concepts about judgment collection you have just learned to real-life situations, before you take the big step to collecting your own judgment.

SAMPLE CASE 1

Your friend Chris borrowed $6,000 from you to buy a car. He was going to give back your money first thing Monday morning when the bank opened. Monday morning came and went and no word from Chris. Many months of phone calls later, he finally calls you back and says he's sorry, but he's had money problems and troubles with the car he bought. He offers to make monthly payments of $250 until the $6,000 is paid off. You reluctantly agree. He sends you two checks for $250 each and then disappears. You decide to go to small claims court and give up the excess $500 so you can get in under the court's jurisdiction of $5,000.

You win your case and receive your judgment in the mail about two weeks later. The court awarded you the $5,000 and $50 in costs. A month passes and you haven't heard a word from Chris, your defendant. No money has arrived either. You check with the court and no appeal was filed. Now what?

You think Chris works as a manager of a men's clothing store, but you haven't talked to him in a long time, so he may have changed jobs.

You remember that you gave him the $6,000 by personal check. You contact your bank and request a copy of the front and back of the check. While you are waiting for the copies to arrive, you call the clothing store and ask if Chris still works there. You are told Chris is off that day but he'll be in the next day. Now you have enough information to get started. You know where Chris works and you will soon know where he banks. Time to go get your money!

First, you go after the asset that is the easiest for your debtor to move—the bank account. Since he can change his bank account in under an hour, you decide to go after that before going after his paycheck. It is unlikely Chris will quit his job to avoid paying your judgment, so his paycheck will remain an option for a little while.

As soon as the copies of your check arrive, you see the fingerprint on the front of the $6,000 check, and you know what that means—Chris went straight to your bank and cashed the check. He didn't deposit it into one of his accounts. Dead end. Move on to the next asset.

You remember about the two $250 checks that Chris sent you. Both checks were from the Bank of America. There is a Bank of America right across the street from the clothing shop where Chris works. Is that his branch? Probably.

The next day you head over to the courthouse and request a writ of execution. Since it is a simple form (and inexpensive—it will cost you less than $20 to file it), you park in front of the courthouse, pump $1 in change into the meter, and run in. Ten minutes later, you are out the door and on your way to the sheriff's office down the street. You arrive and ask the deputy for a bank levy. You are again given a simple form and asked for a fee. This time the fee is $30. You have spent a total of $50 and an hour of your time.

A month later you receive a letter from the sheriff's office explaining that the bank levy received $2,800 and your writ is being sent back to the court. You realize that you have only spent a little money and not much of your time and you have collected over half of your money already! Not too bad.

Now, you need to let the court know what has happened so far, so you fill out a Memorandum of Costs on one of the court's standardized forms. You include the fees you spent at the sheriff's department, the filing fee for the writ, and the interest you have earned so far. You make a copy and hand both the original and the copy to your friend Ralph. Ralph mails Chris the copy. He then completes a proof of service and gives it to you. You file your copy of the Memorandum of Costs and your proof of service down at the courthouse.

While you are back at the courthouse, you get another writ of execution issued. This one has the updated amounts, including the credit you received of $2,800 and the costs you incurred of $50. Minutes later, you head back to the sheriff's office with your writ and ask the deputy for a wage garnishment. You fill out another simple form and pay another fee of $30.

A month later you receive a letter from the sheriff explaining he has received the first of your payments in the amount of $602 (25% of the debtor's gross monthly income) and it will be sent to you shortly.

After several months, you receive the last payment from the wage garnishment. You file a satisfaction of judgment with the court and send a copy to Chris, your debtor. Case closed.

SAMPLE CASE 2

You purchased a new vacuum from Sally's Hardware down the street from your house. Unfortunately, it stopped working after only two days. You call Sally to explain what happened, but she said, "Tough luck." After several unsuccessful rounds of mediation, you ended up in small claims court. The judge awarded you a judgment for the full amount of the vacuum (an industrial shop vacuum) and the court costs, for a total of $1,500.

You wait patiently for Sally to send you the money. The thirty-day period that your state allows for your debtor to file an appeal passes with no word from Sally or the court. Now it is time for you to collect your money.

You would still like to be nice about this, so you write Sally a demand letter. You let her know that her time to appeal has passed and you would like her to send you the money she owes. You give her two weeks to come up with the money, but still hear no word.

Armed with a pen and a pad of paper, you sit down to figure out how this collection thing is supposed to work. You paid for the vacuum with cash and it is the only thing other than nails and some glue that you have ever purchased from Sally. You do not know where she banks. She's self-employed (a sole proprietor), so she's not getting any wages for you to garnish. You know her business is pretty steady, especially on that day you were there. It was a Saturday. She is really busy on Saturdays! She clearly has a cash flow coming in to her business.

You look up your court's website to see what types of procedures are available in your state to help you collect your money and find that till taps and keepers are both available. If you hire the sheriff's department to do the till tap, they may go out first thing in the morning and not get much from the cash register. You figure the keeper will be a better way to go. If the sheriff's deputy stays in the store all day, taking all the cash and checks that come in the door, you should get your money back by the end of the day.

You head down to the courthouse to get a writ of execution. You complete the form and return it to the clerk. You know which county the hardware store is located in, so you have the writ issued to the sheriff of that county. After only a few minutes in line, you leave the courthouse with a writ in hand. You head immediately to the sheriff's office to get a keeper levy.

A few weeks pass, and you get a notice from the sheriff's department that the keeper was successful. The deputy was able to collect your judgment and your costs. As soon as you receive your money from the sheriff, you make your last trip to the courthouse and file an acknowledgment of satisfaction of judgment. You send Sally a copy and keep a copy for yourself. Case closed.

Appendix B:
State Form Websites

To locate forms available in your state, visit the website located next to the name of your state. Many states only provide a limited number of standardized legal forms.

Alabama   www.judicial.state.al.us

Alaska   www.state.ak.us/courts/forms.htm

Arizona   www.superiorcourt.maricopa.gov/
ssc/forms/forms_available.asp

Arkansas   http://courts.state.ar.us/courts/aoc_forms.html

California   www.courtinfo.ca.gov/forms

Colorado	www.courts.state.co.us/chs/court/ forms/garnishmentforms/garnishments.htm
Connecticut	www.jud2.ct.gov/webforms
Delaware	www.municipalcourt.org/scframe.asp
District of Columbia	www.dccourts.gov/dccourts/superior/civil/forms.jsp
Florida	http://smallclaims.homestead.com (Rule 7.341 and 7.342)
Georgia	www.georgiacourts.org/magistrate.html (Limited forms available)
Hawaii	www.courts.state.hi.us
Idaho	www.courtselfhelp.idaho.gov/misc.asp (Limited forms available)
Illinois	www.19thcircuitcourt.state.il.us/ self-help/s_claims/after_the_judgment.htm
Indiana	www.in.gov/judiciary/selfservice/forms.html (Limited forms available)
Iowa	www.judicial.state.ia.us/Court_Rules_and_Forms (Limited forms available)
Kansas	www.kscourts.org/dstcts/4forms.htm

Kentucky	www.courts.ky.gov/forms/formslibrarybycategory.htm
Louisiana	www.brgov.com/dept/citycourt/interforms.htm (County-specific forms—sample)
Maine	www.courts.state.me.us/rules_forms_fees/pub_forms.html
Maryland	www.courts.state.md.us/district/dctcivforms.html
Massachusetts	www.lawlib.state.ma.us/formsm-z.html
Michigan	www.courts.michigan.gov/scao/courtforms/#forms
Minnesota	www.courts.state.mn.us
Mississippi	www.mssd.uscourts.gov/forms.htm (Limited forms available)
Missouri	www.courts.mo.gov
Montana	www.courts.mt.gov/library/topics/judgement.asp
Nebraska	www.supremecourt.ne.gov/forms (Limited forms available)
Nevada	www.co.clark.nv.us/justicecourt_lv/forms.htm
New Hampshire	www.courts.state.nh.us (Limited forms available—mostly Family Law and Probate)

New Jersey	www.judiciary.state.nj.us/forms.htm (Limited forms available)
New Mexico	www.supremecourt.nm.org
New York	www.nycourts.gov/forms/index.shtml#LS (Limited forms available)
North Carolina	www.nccourts.org/Forms/FormSearchResults.asp (Limited forms available)
North Dakota	www.ndcourts.com/court/forms
Ohio	www.cco.state.oh.us (Limited forms available)
Oklahoma	www.oscn.net/static/forms/AOCforms.asp
Oregon	www.ojd.state.or.us/programs/utcr/UTCRForms.htm (Limited forms available)
Pennsylvania	www.courts.state.pa.us
Puerto Rico	www.prd.uscourts.gov/USDCPR/a_forms.htm
Rhode Island	www.courts.state.ri.us/home/forms.htm (Limited forms available)
South Carolina	www.judicial.state.sc.us/forms (Limited forms available)

South Dakota	www.sdjudicial.com (Limited forms available)
Tennessee	www.tsc.state.tn.us
Texas	www.courts.state.tx.us/pubs/pubs-home.asp (Limited forms available)
Utah	www.utcourts.gov/resources/forms
Vermont	www.vermontjudiciary.org/eforms/default.aspx
Virginia	www.courts.state.va.us/forms/district/civil.html
Washington	www.courts.wa.gov/forms/index.cfm
West Virginia	www.state.wv.us/wvsca/rules/formsindex.htm
Wisconsin	www.wicourts.gov/forms1/circuit.htm
Wyoming	www.uintacounty.com (County-specific forms—limited forms available)

The National Center for State Courts' website has a comprehensive list of forms available, by state, for self-represented litigants.
www.ncsconline.org

Appendix C: Sample, Filled-In Forms

This appendix contains filled-in forms for a sample case in California. The forms for collecting a judgment are different for each state, so blank versions of these forms are not provided. However, the forms are similar enough from state to state that these samples should prove helpful when you fill out forms from your own state for your own judgment.

ATTORNEY OR PARTY WITHOUT ATTORNEY *(Name and Address):*   TELEPHONE NO.:

FOR COURT USE ONLY

Robin Plaintiff
123 Smith Street
Big City, CA 94444

ATTORNEY FOR *(Name):*

NAME OF COURT:
STREET ADDRESS: Superior Court of Big City
MAILING ADDRESS: 222 Justice Way
CITY AND ZIP CODE: Big City, CA 94444
BRANCH NAME:

PLAINTIFF: Robin Plaintiff

DEFENDANT: Joe Defendant

CASE NUMBER:

NOTICE OF ENTRY OF JUDGMENT ON SISTER-STATE JUDGMENT

1. TO JUDGMENT DEBTOR *(name):* Joe Defendant

2. YOU ARE NOTIFIED
   a. Upon application of the judgment creditor, a judgment against you has been entered in this court as follows:
      (1) Judgment creditor *(name):* Robin Plaintiff

      (2) Amount of judgment entered in this court: $5000.00

   b. This judgment was entered based upon a sister-state judgment previously entered against you as follows:

      (1) Sister state *(name):* Arizona

      (2) Sister-state court *(name and location):* Superior Court of Desert City, Desert City, AZ 71040

      (3) Judgment entered in sister state on *(date):* 6/25/98

      (4) Title of case and case number *(specify):* Plaintiff vs. Defendant 129654

3. | **A sister-state judgment has been entered against you in a California court. Unless you file a motion to vacate the judgment in this court within 30 DAYS after service of this notice, this judgment will be final.**

   This court may order that a writ of execution or other enforcement may issue. Your wages, money, and property could be taken without further warning from the court.

   If enforcement procedures have already been issued, the property levied on will not be distributed until 30 days after you are served with this notice.

Date: _____   Clerk, by _____, Deputy

4. [ ] NOTICE TO THE PERSON SERVED: You are served
   a. [ ] as an individual judgment debtor.
   b. [ ] under the fictitious name of *(specify):*

   c. [ ] on behalf of *(specify):*

[SEAL]

Under:
[ ] CCP 416.10 (corporation)
[ ] CCP 416.20 (defunct corporation)
[ ] CCP 416.40 (association or partnership)
[ ] other:

[ ] CCP 416.60 (minor)
[ ] CCP 416.70 (conservatee)
[ ] CCP 416.90 (individual)

(Proof of service on reverse)

Form Approved by the
Judicial Council of California
EJ-110 [Rev. July 1, 1983]

**NOTICE OF ENTRY OF JUDGMENT ON
SISTER-STATE JUDGMENT**

CCP 1710.30, 1710.40
1710.45
American LegalNet, Inc.
www.USCourtForms.com

PROOF OF SERVICE
(Use separate proof of service for each person served)

1. I served the Notice of Entry of Judgment on Sister-State Judgment as follows:
   a. on judgment debtor *(name)*: Joe Defendant

   b. by serving   ☒ judgment debtor   ☐ other *(name and title or relationship to person served)*:

   c. ☒ by delivery ☒ at home ☐ at business
      (1) date: 11/10/98
      (2) time: 9:00 A.M.
      (3) address: 228 Jackson Avenue Bit City, CA 9443

   d. ☐ by mailing
      (1) date:
      (2) place:

2. Manner of service *(check proper box)*:
   a. ☒ **Personal service.** By personally delivering copies. (CCP 415.10)
   b. ☐ **Substituted service on corporation, unincorporated association (including partnership), or public entity.** By leaving, during usual office hours, copies in the office of the person served with the person who apparently was in charge and thereafter mailing (by first-class mail, postage prepaid) copies to the person served at the place where the copies were left. (CCP 415.20(a))
   c. ☐ **Substituted service on natural person, minor, conservatee, or candidate.** By leaving copies at the dwelling house, usual place of abode, or usual place of business of the person served in the presence of a competent member of the household or a person apparently in charge of the office or place of business, at least 18 years of age, who was informed of the general nature of the papers, and thereafter mailing (by first-class mail, postage prepaid) copies to the person served at the place where the copies were left. (CCP 415.20(b)) *(Attach separate declaration or affidavit stating acts relied on to establish reasonable diligence in first attempting personal service.)*
   d. ☐ **Mail and acknowledgment service.** By mailing (by first-class mail or airmail, postage prepaid) copies to the person served, together with two copies of the form of notice and acknowledgment and a return envelope, postage prepaid, addressed to the sender. (CCP 415.30) *(Attach completed acknowledgment of receipt.)*
   e. ☐ **Certified or registered mail service.** By mailing to an address outside California (by first-class mail, postage prepaid, requiring a return receipt) copies to the person served. (CCP 415.40) *(Attach signed return receipt or other evidence of actual delivery to the person served.)*
   f. ☐ Other *(specify code section)*:
      ☐ Additional page is attached.

3. The "Notice to the Person Served" was completed as follows:
   a. ☒ as an individual judgment debtor.
   b. ☐ as the person sued under the fictitious name of *(specify)*:
   c. ☐ on behalf of *(specify)*:
      under: ☐ CCP 416.10 (corporation)   ☐ CCP 416.60 (minor)   ☐ other:
         ☐ CCP 416.20 (defunct corporation)   ☐ CCP 416.70 (conservatee)
         ☐ CCP 416.40 (association or partnership)   ☐ CCP 416.90 (individual)

4. At the time of service I was at least 18 years of age and not a party to this action.
5. Fee for service: $ 10.00
6. Person serving:
   a. ☐ California sheriff, marshal, or constable.
   b. ☐ Registered California process server.
   c. ☐ Employee or independent contractor of a registered California process server.
   d. ☒ Not a registered California process server.
   e. ☐ Exempt from registration under Bus. & Prof. Code 22350(b).

   f. Name, address and telephone number and, if applicable, county of registration and number:

I declare under penalty of perjury under the laws of the State of California that the foregoing is true and correct.

(For California sheriff, marshal, or constable use only)
I certify that the foregoing is true and correct.

Date: 11/16/98

Date:

▶ *Bobby Neighbor*
     (SIGNATURE)

▶ _____
     (SIGNATURE)

[EJ-110]

MC-030

ATTORNEY OR PARTY WITHOUT ATTORNEY *(Name, State Bar number, and address)*:	FOR COURT USE ONLY

Robin Plaintiff
123 Smith Street
Big City, CA 94444

TELEPHONE NO.:   FAX NO. *(Optional)*:
E-MAIL ADDRESS *(Optional)*:
ATTORNEY FOR *(Name)*:

SUPERIOR COURT OF CALIFORNIA, COUNTY OF
STREET ADDRESS: Superior Court of Big City
MAILING ADDRESS: 222 Justice Way
CITY AND ZIP CODE: Big City, CA 94444
BRANCH NAME:

PLAINTIFF/PETITIONER: Robin Plaintiff

DEFENDANT/RESPONDENT: Joe Defendant

DECLARATION	CASE NUMBER: 741827

Please change defendant's address from

227 Jackson Avenue
Big City, CA 94443

To:
228 Jackson Avenue
Big City, CA 94443

I declare under penalty of perjury under the laws of the State of California that the foregoing is true and correct.

Date: 12/28/06

_____
Robin Plaintiff
(TYPE OR PRINT NAME)

Robin Plaintiff
_____
(SIGNATURE OF DECLARANT)

☐ Attorney for ☒ Plaintiff ☐ Petitioner ☐ Defendant
☐ Respondent ☐ Other *(Specify)*:

Form Approved for Optional Use
Judicial Council of California
MC-030 [Rev. January 1, 2006]

DECLARATION

Page 1 of 1
American LegalNet, Inc.
www.USCourtForms.com

EJ-190

ATTORNEY OR PARTY WITHOUT ATTORNEY *(Name and Address)*:   TEL NO.:

☐ Recording requested by and return to:

Robin Plaintiff
123 Smith Street
Big City, CA 94444

☐ ATTORNEY FOR   ☒ JUDGMENT CREDITOR   ☐ ASSIGNEE OF RECORD

NAME OF COURT: Superior Court of Big City
STREET ADDRESS: 222 Justice Way
MAILING ADDRESS: Big City, CA 94444
CITY AND ZIP CODE:
BRANCH NAME:

FOR RECORDER'S USE ONLY

CASE NUMBER:

741827

PLAINTIFF: Robin Plaintiff

DEFENDANT: Joe Defendant

FOR COURT USE ONLY

APPLICATION FOR AND RENEWAL OF JUDGMENT

☒ Judgment creditor
☐ Assignee of record
    applies for renewal of the judgment as follows:

1. Applicant *(name and address)*:   Robin Plaintiff
                                  123 Smith Street
                                    Big City, CA 94444

2. Judgment debtor *(name and last known address)*:
                                    Joe Defendant
                                    228 Jackson Avenue
                                    Big City, CA 94443

3. Original judgment
   a. Case number *(specify)*: 741827
   b. Entered on *(date)*: 1/1/98
   c. Recorded:
     (1) Date:
     (2) County:
     (3) Instrument No.:

4. ☐ Judgment previously renewed *(specify each case number and date)*:

5. ☒ Renewal of money judgment
   a. Total judgment . . . . $ 5000.00
   b. Costs after judgment . . . . $ 400.00
   c. Subtotal *(add a and b)* . . . . $ 5400.00
   d. Credits after judgment . . . . $ 0
   e. Subtotal *(subtract d from c)* . . . . $ 5400.00
   f. Interest after judgment . . . . $ 4000.00
   g. Fee for filing renewal application . . . . $ 25.00
   h. **Total renewed judgment** *(add e, f, and g)* . $ 9425.00

   i. ☐ The amounts called for in items a – h are different for each debtor.
         These amounts are stated for each debtor on Attachment 5.

Page 1 of 2

APPLICATION FOR AND RENEWAL OF JUDGMENT

Code of Civil Procedure, § 683.140

American LegalNet, Inc.
www.USCourtForms.com

SHORT TITLE:	CASE NUMBER:
Plaintiff vs. Defendant	741827

6. ☐ Renewal of judgment for ☐ possession.
☐ sale.

   a. ☐ If judgment was not previously renewed, terms of judgment as entered:

   b. ☐ If judgment was previously renewed, terms of judgment as last renewed:

   c. ☐ Terms of judgment remaining unsatisfied:

I declare under penalty of perjury under the laws of the State of California that the foregoing is true and correct.

Date: 1/2/07

Robin Plaintiff	▶ *Robin Plaintiff*
(TYPE OR PRINT NAME)	(SIGNATURE OF DECLARANT)

EJ-195

ATTORNEY OR PARTY WITHOUT ATTORNEY *(Name and Address)*	TELEPHONE NO.:	FOR COURT USE ONLY

Robin Plaintiff
123 Smith Street
Big City, CA 94444

ATTORNEY FOR *(Name)*:

NAME OF COURT:
STREET ADDRESS: Superior Court of Big City
MAILING ADDRESS: 222 Justice Way
CITY AND ZIP CODE: Big City, CA 94444
BRANCH NAME:

PLAINTIFF: Robin Plaintiff

DEFENDANT: Joe Defendant

NOTICE OF RENEWAL OF JUDGMENT

CASE NUMBER:
741827

TO JUDGMENT DEBTOR *(name):* Joe Defendant

1. **This renewal extends** the period of enforceability of the judgment until 10 years from the date the application for renewal was filed.

2. **If you object** to this renewal, you may make a motion to vacate or modify the renewal with this court.

3. You must make this motion within **30 days** after service of this notice on you.

4. A copy of the *Application for and Renewal of Judgment* is attached (*Cal. Rules of Court, rule 3.1900*).

Date:

Clerk, by _____ , Deputy

[SEAL]

See CCP 683.160 for information on method of service

Form Adopted for Mandatory Use
Judicial Council of California
EJ-195 [Rev. January 1, 2007]

NOTICE OF RENEWAL OF JUDGMENT

Code of Civil Procedure, § 683.160
www.courtinfo.ca.gov

American LegalNet, Inc.
www.FormsWorkflow.com

EJ-130

ATTORNEY OR PARTY WITHOUT ATTORNEY *(Name, State Bar number and address)*:	FOR COURT USE ONLY

Robin Plaintiff
123 Smith Street
Big City, CA 94444

TELEPHONE NO.:   FAX NO. *(Optional)*:
E-MAIL ADDRESS *(Optional)*:
ATTORNEY FOR *(Name)*:

☐ ATTORNEY FOR   ☒ JUDGMENT CREDITOR   ☐ ASSIGNEE OF RECORD

SUPERIOR COURT OF CALIFORNIA, COUNTY OF
STREET ADDRESS: Superior Court of Big City
MAILING ADDRESS: 222 Justice Way
CITY AND ZIP CODE: Big City, CA 94444
BRANCH NAME:

PLAINTIFF: Robin Plaintiff

DEFENDANT: Joe Defendant

WRIT OF	☒ EXECUTION (Money Judgment) ☐ POSSESSION OF ☐ Personal Property ☐ Real Property ☐ SALE	CASE NUMBER: 741827

1. **To the Sheriff or Marshal of the County of:** Big City
   You are directed to enforce the judgment described below with daily interest and your costs as provided by law.

2. **To any registered process server:** You are authorized to serve this writ only in accord with CCP 699.080 or CCP 715.040.

3. *(Name):* Robin Plaintiff
   is the ☒ judgment creditor ☐ assignee of record   whose address is shown on this form above the court's name.

4. **Judgment debtor** *(name and last known address):*

   Joe Defendant
   228 Jackson Avenue
   Big City, CA 94443

   ☐ Additional judgment debtors on next page

5. **Judgment entered** on *(date):* 1/1/98

6. ☒ **Judgment renewed** on *(dates):* 1/2/07

7. **Notice of sale** under this writ
   a. ☒ has not been requested.
   b. ☐ has been requested *(see next page).*

8. ☐ Joint debtor information on next page.

   [SEAL]

9. ☐ See next page for information on real or personal property to be delivered under a writ of possession or sold under a writ of sale.
10. ☐ This writ is issued on a sister-state judgment.
11. Total judgment .... $ 9425.00
12. Costs after judgment (per filed order or memo CCP 685.090) .... $ 0
13. Subtotal *(add 11 and 12)* .... $ 9425.00
14. Credits .... $ 0
15. Subtotal *(subtract 14 from 13)* ...... $ 9425.00
16. Interest after judgment (per filed affidavit CCP 685.050) (not on GC 6103.5 fees)... $ 0
17. Fee for issuance of writ .... $ 15.00
18. **Total** *(add 15, 16, and 17)* .... $ 9440.00
19. Levying officer:
    (a) Add daily interest from date of writ *(at the legal rate on 15)* (not on GC 6103.5 fees) of. . . . . . $
    (b) Pay directly to court costs included in 11 and 17 (GC 6103.5, 68511.3; CCP 699.520(i)) .... $
20. ☐ The amounts called for in items 11–19 are different for each debtor. These amounts are stated for each debtor on Attachment 20.

Issued on *(date):* _____ Clerk, by _____, Deputy

NOTICE TO PERSON SERVED: SEE NEXT PAGE FOR IMPORTANT INFORMATION.

Page 1 of 2

Form Approved for Optional Use
Judicial Council of California
EJ-130 [Rev. January 1, 2006]

WRIT OF EXECUTION

Code of Civil Procedure, §§ 699.520, 712.010, Government Code, § 6103.5
www.courtinfo.ca.gov
American LegalNet, Inc.
www.USCourtForms.com

<table>
<tr><td colspan="2"></td><td align="right">**EJ-130**</td></tr>
<tr><td>PLAINTIFF: Robin Plaintiff</td><td>CASE NUMBER:</td></tr>
<tr><td>DEFENDANT: Joe Defendant</td><td>741827</td></tr>
</table>

— Items continued from page 1 —

21. ☐ **Additional judgment debtor** *(name and last known address):*

22. ☐ **Notice of sale** has been requested by *(name and address):*

23. ☐ **Joint debtor** was declared bound by the judgment (CCP 989–994)
    a. on *(date):*   a. on *(date):*
    b. name and address of joint debtor: b. name and address of joint debtor:

    c. ☐ additional costs against certain joint debtors *(itemize):*

24. ☐ *(Writ of Possession* or *Writ of Sale)* **Judgment** was entered for the following:
    a. ☐ Possession of real property: The complaint was filed on *(date):*
        (Check (1) or (2)):
        (1) ☐ The Prejudgment Claim of Right to Possession was served in compliance with CCP 415.46.
             The judgment includes all tenants, subtenants, named claimants, and other occupants of the premises.
        (2) ☐ The Prejudgment Claim of Right to Possession was NOT served in compliance with CCP 415.46.
             (a) $ was the daily rental value on the date the complaint was filed.
             (b) The court will hear objections to enforcement of the judgment under CCP 1174.3 on the following
                 dates *(specify):*
    b. ☐ Possession of personal property.
        ☐ If delivery cannot be had, then for the value *(itemize in 9e)* specified in the judgment or supplemental order.
    c. ☐ Sale of personal property.
    d. ☐ Sale of real property.
    e. Description of property:

NOTICE TO PERSON SERVED

WRIT OF EXECUTION OR SALE. Your rights and duties are indicated on the accompanying *Notice of Levy* (Form EJ-150).
WRIT OF POSSESSION OF PERSONAL PROPERTY. If the levying officer is not able to take custody of the property, the levying officer will make a demand upon you for the property. If custody is not obtained following demand, the judgment may be enforced as a money judgment for the value of the property specified in the judgment or in a supplemental order.
WRIT OF POSSESSION OF REAL PROPERTY. If the premises are not vacated within five days after the date of service on the occupant or, if service is by posting, within five days after service on you, the levying officer will remove the occupants from the real property and place the judgment creditor in possession of the property. Except for a mobile home, personal property remaining on the premises will be sold or otherwise disposed of in accordance with CCP 1174 unless you or the owner of the property pays the judgment creditor the reasonable cost of storage and takes possession of the personal property not later than 15 days after the time the judgment creditor takes possession of the premises.
► A Claim of Right to Possession form accompanies this writ *(unless the Summons was served in compliance with CCP 415.46).*

EJ-130 [Rev. January 1, 2006]   **WRIT OF EXECUTION**   Page 2 of 2

MC-012

ATTORNEY OR PARTY WITHOUT ATTORNEY *(Name, state bar number, and address)*:	FOR COURT USE ONLY
Robin Plaintiff 123 Smith Street Big City, CA 94444 TELEPHONE NO.:　　　　　　　FAX NO.: ATTORNEY FOR *(Name)*:	

NAME OF COURT: Superior Court of Big City
STREET ADDRESS: 222 Justice Way
MAILING ADDRESS:
CITY AND ZIP CODE: Big City, CA 94444
BRANCH NAME:

PLAINTIFF: Robin Plaintiff

DEFENDANT: Joe Defendant

MEMORANDUM OF COSTS AFTER JUDGMENT, ACKNOWLEDGMENT OF CREDIT, AND DECLARATION OF ACCRUED INTEREST	CASE NUMBER: 741827

1. I claim the following costs after judgment incurred within the last two years *(indicate if there are multiple items in any category)*:

		Dates Incurred	Amount
a	Preparing and issuing abstract of judgment		$
b	Recording and indexing abstract of judgment		$
c	Filing notice of judgment lien on personal property		$
d	Issuing writ of execution, to extent not satisfied by Code Civ. Proc., § 685.050 *(specify county)*:		$
e	Levying officer's fees, to extent not satisfied by Code Civ. Proc., § 685.050 or wage garnishment	11/9/06	$ 100.00
f	Approved fee on application for order for appearance of judgment debtor, or other approved costs under Code Civ. Proc., § 708.010 et seq.		$
g	Attorney fees, if allowed by Code Civ. Proc., § 685.040		$
h	Other: Private Investigator *(Statute authorizing cost)*:	685.040	$ 30.00
i	Total of claimed costs for current memorandum of costs *(add items a-h)*		$

2. All previously allowed postjudgment costs: . . . . $ 270.00

3. **Total** of all postjudgment costs *(add items 1 and 2)*: . . . .**TOTAL** $ 400.00

4. **Acknowledgment of Credit.** I acknowledge total credit to date (including returns on levy process and direct payments) in the amount of: $ 0

5. **Declaration of Accrued Interest.** Interest on the judgment accruing at the legal rate from the date of entry on balances due after partial satisfactions and other credits in the amount of: $ 400.00

6. I am the ☒ judgment creditor ☐ agent for the judgment creditor ☐ attorney for the judgment creditor.
I have knowledge of the facts concerning the costs claimed above. To the best of my knowledge and belief, the costs claimed are correct, reasonable, and necessary, and have not been satisfied.

I declare under penalty of perjury under the laws of the State of California that the foregoing is true and correct.

Date: 1/2/07

. . . . Robin Plaintiff . . . .
(TYPE OR PRINT NAME)

▶ *Robin Plaintiff*
(SIGNATURE OF DECLARANT)

NOTICE TO THE JUDGMENT DEBTOR
If this memorandum of costs is filed at the same time as an application for a writ of execution, any statutory costs, *not exceeding $100 in aggregate* and not already allowed by the court, may be included in the writ of execution. *The fees sought under this memorandum may be disallowed by the court upon a motion to tax filed by the debtor, notwithstanding the fees having been included in the writ of execution.* (Code Civ. Proc., § 685.070(e).) A motion to tax costs claimed in this memorandum must be filed within 10 days after service of the memorandum. (Code Civ. Proc., § 685.070(c).)

(Proof of service on reverse)

Form Adopted for Mandatory Use Judicial Council of California MC-012 [Rev January 1, 2000]	MEMORANDUM OF COSTS AFTER JUDGMENT, ACKNOWLEDGMENT OF CREDIT, AND DECLARATION OF ACCRUED INTEREST	Code of Civil Procedure, § 685.070 American LegalNet, Inc. www.USCourtForms.com

190

<table>
<tr><td>SHORT TITLE:

    Plaintiff vs. Defendant</td><td>CASE NUMBER:

741827</td></tr>
</table>

PROOF OF SERVICE
☒ **Mail**   ☐ **Personal Service**

1. At the time of service I was at least 18 years of age and **not a party to this legal action.**

2. My residence or business address is (specify): 122 Smith Street
   Big City, CA 94444

3. I mailed or personally delivered a copy of the *Memorandum of Costs After Judgment, Acknowledgment of Credit, and Declaration of Accrued Interest* as follows *(complete either a or b):*

   a. ☒ **Mail.** I am a resident of or employed in the county where the mailing occurred.
      (1) I enclosed a copy in an envelope AND
        (a) ☒ **deposited** the sealed envelope with the United States Postal Service with the postage fully prepaid.
        (b) ☐ **placed** the envelope for collection and mailing on the date and at the place shown in items below following our ordinary business practices. I am readily familiar with this business's practice for collecting and processing correspondence for mailing. On the same day that correspondence is placed for collection and mailing, it is deposited in the ordinary course of business with the United States Postal Service in a sealed envelope with postage fully prepaid.
      (2) The envelope was addressed and mailed as follows:
        (a) Name of person served: Joe Defendant
        (b) Address on envelope: 228 Jackson Avenue
                      Big City, CA 94443

        (c) Date of mailing: 1/3/07
        (d) Place of mailing (city and state): Big City, CA 94443

   b. ☐ **Personal delivery.** I personally delivered a copy as follows:
      (1) Name of person served:
      (2) Address where delivered:

      (3) Date delivered:
      (4) Time delivered:

I declare under penalty of perjury under the laws of the State of California that the foregoing is true and correct.

Date: 1/3/07

Bobby Neighbor
(TYPE OR PRINT NAME)

▶ *Bobby Neighbor*
(SIGNATURE OF DECLARANT)

AT-138, EJ-125

ATTORNEY OR PARTY WITHOUT ATTORNEY *(Name, state bar number, and address)*:	FOR COURT USE ONLY
Robin Plaintiff 123 Smith Street Big City, CA 94444 TELEPHONE NO.: FAX NO.: ATTORNEY FOR *(Name)*:	

NAME OF COURT: Superior Court of Big City
STREET ADDRESS: 222 Justice Way
MAILING ADDRESS:
CITY AND ZIP CODE: Big City, CA 94444
BRANCH NAME:

PLAINTIFF: Robin Plaintiff

DEFENDANT: Joe Defendant

APPLICATION AND ORDER FOR APPEARANCE AND EXAMINATION	CASE NUMBER:
☒ **ENFORCEMENT OF JUDGMENT** ☐ **ATTACHMENT (Third Person)** ☐ Judgment Debtor ☒ Third Person	741827

ORDER TO APPEAR FOR EXAMINATION

1. TO *(name)*: Joe Defendant
2. YOU ARE ORDERED TO APPEAR personally before this court, or before a referee appointed by the court, to
   a. ☐ furnish information to aid in enforcement of a money judgment against you.
   b. ☒ answer concerning property of the judgment debtor in your possession or control or concerning a debt you owe the judgment debtor.
   c. ☐ answer concerning property of the defendant in your possession or control or concerning a debt you owe the defendant that is subject to attachment.

   Date: 2/15/07   Time: 9:00 A.M.   Dept. or Div.: 610   Rm.: 610
   Address of court ☒ shown above ☐ is:

3. This order may be served by a sheriff, marshal, registered process server, **or** the following specially appointed person *(name)*:

   Date: _____
                                                            JUDGE OR REFEREE

This order must be served not less than 10 days before the date set for the examination.
IMPORTANT NOTICES ON REVERSE

APPLICATION FOR ORDER TO APPEAR FOR EXAMINATION

4. ☒ Judgment creditor   ☐ Assignee of record   ☐ Plaintiff who has a right to attach order
   applies for an order requiring *(name)*:   to appear and furnish information
   to aid in enforcement of the money judgment or to answer concerning property or debt.

5. The person to be examined is
   a. ☐ the judgment debtor.
   b. ☒ a third person (1) who has possession or control of property belonging to the judgment debtor or the defendant or (2) who owes the judgment debtor or the defendant more than $250. An affidavit supporting this application under Code of Civil Procedure section 491.110 or 708.120 is attached.

6. The person to be examined resides or has a place of business in this county or within 150 miles of the place of examination.

7. ☐ This court is **not** the court in which the money judgment is entered or *(attachment only)* the court that issued the writ of attachment. An affidavit supporting an application under Code of Civil Procedure section 491.150 or 708.160 is attached.

8. ☐ The judgment debtor has been examined within the past 120 days. An affidavit showing good cause for another examination is attached.

I declare under penalty of perjury under the laws of the State of California that the foregoing is true and correct.

Date: 1/10/07

Robin Plaintiff   ▶ *Robin Plaintiff*
(TYPE OR PRINT NAME)   (SIGNATURE OF DECLARANT)

(Continued on reverse)

Form Adopted for Mandatory Use
Judicial Council of California
AT-138, EJ-125 [Rev. July 1, 2000]

**APPLICATION AND ORDER
FOR APPEARANCE AND EXAMINATION**
(Attachment—Enforcement of Judgment)

Code of Civil Procedure,
§§ 491.110, 708.110, 708.120

American LegalNet, Inc.
www.USCourtForms.com

APPEARANCE OF JUDGMENT DEBTOR (ENFORCEMENT OF JUDGMENT)

NOTICE TO JUDGMENT DEBTOR If you fail to appear at the time and place specified in this order, you may be subject to arrest and punishment for contempt of court, and the court may make an order requiring you to pay the reasonable attorney fees incurred by the judgment creditor in this proceeding.

APPEARANCE OF A THIRD PERSON
(ENFORCEMENT OF JUDGMENT)

(1) NOTICE TO PERSON SERVED If you fail to appear at the time and place specified in this order, you may be subject to arrest and punishment for contempt of court, and the court may make an order requiring you to pay the reasonable attorney fees incurred by the judgment creditor in this proceeding.

(2) NOTICE TO JUDGMENT DEBTOR The person in whose favor the judgment was entered in this action claims that the person to be examined pursuant to this order has possession or control of property which is yours or owes you a debt. This property or debt is as follows *(Describe the property or debt using typewritten capital letters)*:

If you claim that all or any portion of this property or debt is exempt from enforcement of the money judgment, you must file your exemption claim in writing with the court and have a copy personally served on the judgment creditor not later than three days before the date set for the examination. You must appear at the time and place set for the examination to establish your claim of exemption or your exemption may be waived.

APPEARANCE OF A THIRD PERSON (ATTACHMENT)

NOTICE TO PERSON SERVED If you fail to appear at the time and place specified in this order, you may be subject to arrest and punishment for contempt of court, and the court may make an order requiring you to pay the reasonable attorney fees incurred by the plaintiff in this proceeding.

APPEARANCE OF A CORPORATION, PARTNERSHIP,
ASSOCIATION, TRUST, OR OTHER ORGANIZATION

It is your duty to designate one or more of the following to appear and be examined: officers, directors, managing agents, or other persons who are familiar with your property and debts.

AT-138, EJ-125 [Rev. July 1, 2000] **APPLICATION AND ORDER
FOR APPEARANCE AND EXAMINATION**
(Attachment—Enforcement of Judgment) | WEST GROUP
Official Publisher | Page two

SC-134

Name and Address of Court:

SMALL CLAIMS CASE NO.: 741827

PLAINTIFF/DE MANDANTE *(Name, street address, and telephone number of each)*:

Robin Plaintiff
123 Smith Street
Big City, CA 94444

Telephone No.:

DEFENDANT/DEMANDADO *(Name, street address, and telephone number of each)*:

Joe Defendant
228 Jackson Avenue
Big City, CA 94443

Telephone No.:

☐ See attached sheet for additional plaintiffs and defendants.

ORDER TO PRODUCE STATEMENT OF ASSETS
AND TO APPEAR FOR EXAMINATION

1. TO JUDGMENT DEBTOR *(name)*: Joe Defendant
2. YOU ARE ORDERED
   a. to pay the judgment and file proof of payment (a canceled check or money order or cash receipt, and a written declaration that shows full payment of the judgment, including postjudgment costs and interest) with the court before the hearing date shown in the box below, **OR**
   b. to (1) personally appear in this court on the date and time shown in the box below, and (2) bring with you a completed *Judgment Debtor's Statement of Assets* (form SC-133). (At the hearing you will be required to explain why you did not complete and mail form SC-133 to judgment creditor within 30 days after the *Notice of Entry of Judgment* (form SC-130) was mailed or handed to you by the clerk, and to answer questions about your income and assets.)

HEARING DATE FECHA DEL JUICIO		DATE	DAY	TIME	PLACE	COURT USE
	1.	2/16/07	FRI	9:00 A.M.	Dept. 612	
	2.					
	3.					

If you fail to appear and have not paid the judgment, including postjudgment costs and interest, a bench warrant may be issued for your arrest, you may be held in contempt of court, and you may be ordered to pay penalties.	Si usted no se presenta y no ha pagado el monto del fallo judicial, inclusive las costas e intereses posterlores al fallo, la corte puede expedir una orden de detencion contra usted, declararle en desacato y ordenar clue pague multas.

3. This order may be served by a sheriff, marshal, or registered process server.

Date: ▶

(SIGNATURE OF JUDGE)

APPLICATION FOR THIS ORDER

A. Judgment creditor (the person who won the case) *(name)*: Robin Plaintiff applies for an order requiring judgment debtor (the person or business who lost the case and owes money) *(name)*: Joe Defendant to (1) pay the judgment or (2) personally appear in this court with a completed *Judgment Debtor's Statement of Assets* (form SC-133), explain why judgment debtor did not pay the judgment or complete and mail form SC-133 to judgment creditor within 30 days after the *Notice of Entry of Judgment* was mailed or handed to judgment debtor, and answer questions about judgment debtor's income and assets.

B. Judgment creditor states the following:
   (1) Judgment debtor has not paid the judgment.
   (2) Judgment debtor either did not file an appeal or the appeal has been dismissed or judgment debtor lost the appeal.
   (3) Judgment debtor either did not file a motion to vacate or the motion to vacate has been denied.
   (4) More than 30 days have passed since the *Notice of Entry of Judgment* form was mailed or delivered to judgment debtor.
   (5) Judgment creditor has not received a completed *Judgment Debtor's Statement of Assets* form from judgment debtor.
   (6) The person to be examined resides or has a place of business in this county or within 150 miles of the place of examination.

I declare under penalty of perjury under the laws of the State of California that the foregoing is true and correct.

Date: 1/10/07

. . . . Robin Plaintiff . . . .
(TYPE OR PRINT NAME)

▶ *Robin Plaintiff*
(DECLARANT)

(See Instructions on reverse)

— The county provides small claims advisor services free of charge. —

Page 1 of 2

Form Adopted for Mandatory Use
Judicial Council of California
SC-134 [Rev. January 1, 2007]

**APPLICATION AND ORDER TO PRODUCE STATEMENT
OF ASSETS AND TO APPEAR FOR EXAMINATION**
(Small Claims)

Code of Civil Procedure §§ 11 6.820,116.830
www.courtinfo.ca.gov

American LegalNet, Inc.
www.FormsWorkflow.com

INSTRUCTIONS FOR JUDGMENT CREDITOR

1. To set a hearing on an *Application for Order to Produce Statement of Assets and to Appear for Examination,* you must complete this form, present it to the court clerk, and pay the fee for an initial hearing date or a reset hearing date.

2. After you file this form, the clerk will set a hearing date, note the hearing date on the form, and return two copies or an original and one copy of the form to you.

3. You must have a copy of this form and a blank copy of the *Judgment Debtor's Statement of Assets* (form SC-133) personally served on the judgment debtor by a sheriff, marshal, or registered process server at least 10 calendar days before the date of the hearing, and have a proof of service filed with the court. The law provides for a new fee if you reset the hearing.

4. If the judgment is paid, including all postjudgment costs and interest, you must immediately complete the *Acknowledgment of Satisfaction of Judgment form* on the reverse of the *Notice of Entry of Judgment* (form SC-130) and file a copy with the court.

5. You must attend the hearing unless the judgment has been paid.

6. This form is intended to be an easy tool to enforce your right to receive a completed *Judgment Debtor's Statement of Assets* (form SC-133). This form is not intended to replace the *Application and Order for Appearance and Examination* (form EJ-125), often called an "Order for Examination." The *Application and Order for Appearance and Examination* may still be used to enforce a small claims judgment if you are not seeking at the same time to make the debtor complete a *Judgment Debtor's Statement of Assets.*

**APPLICATION AND ORDER TO PRODUCE STATEMENT
OF ASSETS AND TO APPEAR FOR EXAMINATION
(Small Claims)**

EJ-001

ATTORNEY OR PARTY WITHOUT ATTORNEY (*Name, address, State Bar number, and telephone number*):
Recording requested by and return to

Robin Plaintiff
123 Smith Street
Big City, CA 94444

☐ ATTORNEY FOR   ☒ JUDGMENT CREDITOR   ☐ ASSIGNEE OF RECORD

SUPERIOR COURT OF CALIFORNIA, COUNTY OF
STREET ADDRESS: Superior Court of Big City
MAILING ADDRESS: 222 Justice Way
CITY AND ZIP CODE: Big City, CA 94444
BRANCH NAME:

FOR RECORDER'S USE ONLY

PLAINTIFF: Robin Plaintiff

DEFENDANT: Joe Defendant

CASE NUMBER:
741827

**ABSTRACT OF JUDGMENT—CIVIL
AND SMALL CLAIMS**   ☐ Amended

FOR COURT USE ONLY

1. The ☒ judgment creditor ☐ assignee of record
applies for an abstract of judgment and represents the following:
a. Judgment debtor's

Name and last known address

Joe Defendant
228 Jackson Avenue
Big City, CA 94443

b. Driver's license No. and state: ☒ Unknown
c. Social security No.: ☒ Unknown
d. Summons or notice of entry of sister-state judgment was personally served or mailed to (*name and address*):

2. ☐ Information on additional judgment debtors is shown on page 2.

3. Judgment creditor (*name and address*):
Robin Plaintiff
123 Smith Street
Big City, CA 94444

Date: 1/10/07

Robin Plaintiff
(TYPE OR PRINT NAME)

4. ☐ Information on additional judgment creditors is shown on page 2.

5. ☐ Original abstract recorded in this county:
a. Date:
b. Instrument No.:

▶ *Robin Plaintiff*
(SIGNATURE OF APPLICANT OR ATTORNEY)

6. Total amount of judgment as entered or last renewed:
$ 9440.00

7. All judgment creditors and debtors are listed on this abstract.

8. a. Judgment entered on (*date*): 1/1/98
b. Renewal entered on (*date*): 1/2/07

9. ☐ This judgment is an installment judgment.

[SEAL]

This abstract issued on (*date*):

10. ☐ An ☒ execution lien ☐ attachment lien
is endorsed on the judgment as follows:
a. Amount: $ 9440.00
b. In favor of (*name and address*):

11. A stay of enforcement has
a. ☒ not been ordered by the court.
b. ☐ been ordered by the court effective until (*date*):

12. a. ☒ I certify that this is a true and correct abstract of the judgment entered in this action.
b. ☐ A certified copy of the judgment is attached.

Clerk, by _____, Deputy

Form Adopted for Mandatory Use
Judicial Council of California
EJ-001 [Rev. January 1, 2006]

**ABSTRACT OF JUDGMENT—CIVIL
AND SMALL CLAIMS**

Code of Civil Procedure, §§ 488.480, 674, 700.190

Page 1 of 2

American LegalNet, Inc.
www.USCourtForms.com

PLAINTIFF: Robin Plaintiff	CASE NUMBER:
DEFENDANT: Joe Defendant	741827

NAMES AND ADDRESSES OF ADDITIONAL JUDGMENT CREDITORS:

13. Judgment creditor *(name and address):*   14. Judgment creditor *(name and address):*

15. ☐ Continued on Attachment 15.

INFORMATION ON ADDITIONAL JUDGMENT DEBTORS:

16.   Name and last known address   17.   Name and last known address

Driver's license No. & state: ☐ Unknown   Driver's license No. & state: ☐ Unknown
Social security No.:   ☐ Unknown   Social security No.:   ☐ Unknown
Summons was personally served at or mailed to *(address):*   Summons was personally served at or mailed to *(address):*

18.   Name and last known address   19.   Name and last known address

Driver's license No. & state: ☐ Unknown   Driver's license No. & state: ☐ Unknown
Social security No.:   ☐ Unknown   Social security No.:   ☐ Unknown
Summons was personally served at or mailed to *(address):*   Summons was personally served at or mailed to *(address):*

20.   Name and last known address   21.   Name and last known address

Driver's license No. & state: ☐ Unknown   Driver's license No. & state: ☐ Unknown
Social security No.:   ☐ Unknown   Social security No.:   ☐ Unknown
Summons was personally served at or mailed to *(address):*   Summons was personally served at or mailed to *(address):*

22. ☐ Continued on Attachment 22.

**ABSTRACT OF JUDGMENT—CIVIL
AND SMALL CLAIMS**

EXEMPTIONS FROM THE ENFORCEMENT OF JUDGMENTS

EJ-155

The following is a list of assets that may be exempt from levy on a judgment.

Exemptions are found in the United States Code (**USC**) and in the California codes, primarily the Code of Civil Procedure (**CCP**).

Because of periodic changes in the law, the list may not include all exemptions that apply in your case. The exemptions may not apply in full or under all circumstances. Some are not available after a certain period of time. You or your attorney should read the statutes.

If you believe the assets that are being levied on are exempt, file a claim of exemption form, which you can get from the levying officer.

> **AMOUNT OF EXEMPTIONS:** A list of the amounts of exemptions from a judgment under CCP § 703.150 starting on April 1, 2004, is available from the clerk of the court and on the California Courts Web site at *www.courtinfo.ca.gov.* Except as otherwise provided, the dollar amounts of the exemptions will be adjusted thereafter at three-year intervals on April 1, and the adjusted amounts will become effective immediately on that date.

Type of Property	Code and Section
Accounts *(See Deposit Accounts)*	
Appliances	CCP § 704.020
Art and Heirlooms	CCP § 704.040
Automobiles	CCP § 704.010
BART District Benefits	CCP § 704.110
	Pub Util C § 28896
Benefit Payments:	
BART District Benefits	CCP § 704.110
	Pub Util C § 28896
Charity	CCP § 704.170
Civil Service Retirement	
Benefits (Federal)	5 USC § 8346
County Employees	
Retirement Benefits	CCP § 704.110
	Govt C § 31452
Disability Insurance Benefits	CCP § 704.130
Fire Service Retirement	
Benefits	CCP § 704.110
	Govt C § 32210
Fraternal Organization	
Funds Benefits	CCP § 704.130
	CCP § 704.170
Health Insurance Benefits	CCP § 704.130
Irrigation System	
Retirement Benefits	CCP § 704.110
Judges Survivors Benefits	
(Federal)	28 USC § 376(n)
Legislators Retirement	
Benefits	CCP § 704.110
	Govt C § 9359.3
Life Insurance Benefits:	
Group	CCP § 704.100
Individual	CCP § 704.100
Lighthouse Keepers	
Widows Benefits	33 USC § 775
Longshore & Harbor Workers	
Compensation or Benefits	33 USC § 916
Military Benefits:	
Retirement	10 USC § 1440
Survivors	10 USC § 1450
Municipal Utility District	
Retirement Benefits	CCP § 704.110
	Pub Util C § 12337
Peace Officers Retirement	
Benefits	CCP § 704.110
	Govt C § 31913
Pension Plans	
(and Death Benefits):	
Private	CCP § 704.115
Public	CCP § 704.110
Public Assistance	CCP § 704.170
	Welf & I C § 17409

Type of Property	Code and Section
Benefit Payments *(cont.)*	
Relocation Benefits	CCP § 704.180
Retirement Benefits	
and Contributions:	
Private	CCP § 704.115
Public	CCP § 704.110
Segregated Benefit Funds	Ins C § 10498.5
Social Security Benefits	42 USC § 407
Strike Benefits	CCP § 704.120
Transit District Retirement	
Benefits (Alameda and	
Contra Costa Counties)	CCP § 704.110
	Pub Util C § 25337
Unemployment Benefits	
and Contributions	CCP § 704.120
Veterans Benefits	38 USC § 3101
Veterans Medal of Honor	
Benefits	38 USC § 562
Welfare Payments	CCP § 704.170
	Welf & I C § 17409
Workers Compensation	CCP § 704.160
Boats	CCP § 704.060
	CCP § 704.710
Books	CCP § 704.060
Building Materials (Residential)	CCP § 704.030
Business:	
Licenses	CCP § 695.060
	CCP § 699.720(a)(1)
Tools of Trade	CCP § 704.060
Cars and Trucks (including	
proceeds)	CCP § 704.010
Cash	CCP § 704.070
Cemeteries:	
Land Proceeds	Health & SC § 7925
Plots	CCP § 704.200
Charity	CCP § 704.170
Claims, Actions and Awards:	
Personal Injury	CCP § 704.140
Worker's Compensation	CCP § 704.160
Wrongful Death	CCP § 704.150
Clothing	CCP § 704.020
Condemnation Proceeds	CCP § 704.720(b)
County Employees Retirement	
Benefits	CCP § 704.110
	Govt C § 31452
Damages *(See Personal Injury*	
and Wrongful Death)	
Deposit Accounts:	
Escrow or Trust Funds	Fin C § 17410
Social Security Direct	
Deposits	CCP § 704.080

Page 1 of 2

Form Approved for Optional Use
Judicial Council of California
EJ-155 [Revised January 1, 2005]

EXEMPTIONS FROM THE ENFORCEMENT OF JUDGMENTS

Code of Civil Procedure,
§§ 681.030(c), 700.010
www.courtinfo.ca.gov

American LegalNet, Inc.
www.USCourtForms.com

EXEMPTIONS FROM THE ENFORCEMENT OF JUDGMENTS
(Continued)

Type of Property	Code and Section
Direct Deposit Account:	
Social Security	CCP § 704.080
Disability Insurance Benefits	CCP § 704.130
Dwelling House	CCP § 704.740
Earnings	CCP § 704.070
	CCP § 706.050
	15 USC § 1673(a)
Educational Grant	Ed C § 21116
Employment Bonds	Lab C § 404
Financial Assistance:	
Charity	CCP § 704.170
Public Assistance	CCP § 704.170
	Welf & I C § 17409
Student Aid	CCP § 704.190
Welfare *(See Public Assistance)*	
Fire Service Retirement	CCP § 704.110
	Govt C § 32210
Fraternal Organizations	
Funds and Benefits	CCP § 704.130
	CCP § 704.170
Fuel for Residence	CCP § 704.020
Furniture	CCP § 704.020
General Assignment for	
Benefit of Creditors	CCP § 1801
Health Aids	CCP § 704.050
Health Insurance Benefits	CCP § 704.130
Home:	
Building Materials	CCP § 704.030
Dwelling House	CCP § 704.740
Homestead	CCP § 704.720
	CCP § 704.730
Housetrailer	CCP § 704.710
Mobilehome	CCP § 704.710
Homestead	CCP § 704.720
	CCP § 704.730
Household Furnishings	CCP § 704.020
Insurance:	
Disability Insurance	CCP § 704.130
Fraternal Benefit Society	CCP § 704.110
Group Life	CCP § 704.100
Health Insurance Benefits	CCP § 704.130
Individual	CCP § 704.100
Insurance Proceeds—	
Motor Vehicle	CCP § 704.010
Irrigation System	CCP § 704.040
Retirement Benefits	CCP § 704.110
Jewelry	
Judges Survivors Benefits	
(Federal)	28 USC § 376(n)
Legislators Retirement	
Benefits	CCP § 704.110
	Govt C § 9359.3
Licenses	CCP § 695.060
	CCP § 720(a)(1)
Lighthouse Keepers Widows	
Benefits	33 USC § 775
Longshore and Harbor Workers	
Compensation or Benefits	33 USC § 916
Military Benefits:	
Retirement	10 USC § 1440
Survivors	10 USC § 1450
Military Personnel—Property	50 USC § 523(b)
Motor Vehicle (Including	
Proceeds)	CCP § 704.010
	CCP § 704.060

Type of Property	Code and Section
Municipal Utility District	
Retirement Benefits	CCP § 704.110
	Pub Util C § 12337
Peace Officers Retirement	
Benefits	CCP § 704.110
	Govt C § 31913
Pension Plans:	
Private	CCP § 704.115
Public	CCP § 704.110
Personal Effects	CCP § 704.020
Personal Injury Actions	
or Damages	CCP § 704.140
Prisoner's Funds	CCP § 704.090
Property Not Subject to	
Enforcement of Money	
Judgments	CCP § 704.210
Prosthetic and Orthopedic	
Devices	CCP § 704.050
Provisions (for Residence)	CCP § 704.020
Public Assistance	CCP § 704.170
	Welf & I C § 17409
Public Employees:	
Death Benefits	CCP § 704.110
Pension	CCP § 704.110
Retirement Benefits	CCP § 704.110
Vacation Credits	CCP § 704.113
Railroad Retirement Benefits	45 USC § 2281
Railroad Unemployment	
Insurance	45 USC § 352(e)
Relocation Benefits	CCP § 704.180
Retirement Benefits and	
Contributions:	
Private	CCP § 704.115
Public	CCP § 704.110
	Ins C § 10498.5
Segregated Benefit Funds	Ins C § 10498.6
Servicemembers Property	50 USC § 523(b)
Social Security	42 USC § 407
Social Security Direct Deposit	
Account	CCP § 704.080
Strike Benefits	CCP § 704.120
Student Aid	CCP § 704.190
Tools of Trade	CCP § 704.060
Transit District Retirement	
Benefits (Alameda and Contra	
Costa Counties)	CCP § 704.110
	Pub Util C § 25337
Travelers Check Sales Proceeds	Fin C § 1875
Unemployment Benefits and	
Contributions	CCP § 704.120
Uniforms	CCP § 704.060
Vacation Credits (Public	
Employees)	CCP § 704.113
Veterans Benefits	38 USC § 3101
Veterans Medal of Honor	
Benefits	38 USC § 562
Wages	CCP § 704.070
	CCP § 706.050
	CCP § 706.051
Welfare Payments	CCP § 704.170
	Welf & I C § 17409
Workers Compensation	
Claims or Awards	CCP § 704.160
Wrongful Death Actions or	
Damages	CCP § 704.150

EXEMPTIONS FROM THE ENFORCEMENT OF JUDGMENTS

SUBP-002

ATTORNEY OR PARTY WITHOUT ATTORNEY *(Name, state bar number, and address)*:	FOR COURT USE ONLY

Robin Plaintiff
123 Smith Street
Big City, CA 94444

TELEPHONE NO.:   FAX NO.:
ATTORNEY FOR *(Name)*:

NAME OF COURT: Superior Court of Big City
STREET ADDRESS: 222 Justice Way
MAILING ADDRESS:
CITY AND ZIP CODE: Big City, CA 94444
BRANCH NAME:

PLAINTIFF/PETITIONER: Robin Plaintiff

DEFENDANT/RESPONDENT: Joe Defendant

CIVIL SUBPOENA (DUCES TECUM) for Personal Appearance and Production of Documents and Things at Trial or Hearing AND DECLARATION	CASE NUMBER: 741827

THE PEOPLE OF THE STATE OF CALIFORNIA, TO *(name, address, and telephone number of witness, if known)*:

Joe Defendant 228 Jackson Avenue Big City, CA 94443

1. YOU ARE ORDERED TO APPEAR AS A WITNESS in this action at the date, time, and place shown in the box below UNLESS your appearance is excused as indicated in box 3b below or you make an agreement with the person named in item 4 below.

> a. Date: 2/16/07   Time: 9:00 A.M.   ☒ Dept.: 612   ☒ Div.: 612   ☒ Room: 612
> b. Address: 222 Justice Way

2. IF YOU HAVE BEEN SERVED WITH THIS SUBPOENA AS A CUSTODIAN OF CONSUMER OR EMPLOYEE RECORDS UNDER CODE OF CIVIL PROCEDURE SECTION 1985.3 OR 1985.6 AND A MOTION TO QUASH OR AN OBJECTION HAS BEEN SERVED ON YOU, A COURT ORDER OR AGREEMENT OF THE PARTIES, WITNESSES, *AND* CONSUMER OR EMPLOYEE AFFECTED MUST BE OBTAINED BEFORE YOU ARE REQUIRED TO PRODUCE CONSUMER OR EMPLOYEE RECORDS.

3. YOU ARE *(item a or b must be checked)*:
   a. ☒ Ordered to appear in person and to produce the records described in the declaration on page two or the attached declaration or affidavit. The personal attendance of the custodian or other qualified witness and the production of the original records are required by this subpoena. The procedure authorized by Evidence Code sections 1560(b), 1561, and 1562 will not be deemed sufficient compliance with this subpoena.
   b. ☐ Not required to appear in person if you produce (i) the records described in the declaration on page two or the attached declaration or affidavit and (ii) a completed declaration of custodian of records in compliance with Evidence Code sections 1560, 1561, 1562, and 1271. (1) Place a copy of the records in an envelope (or other wrapper). Enclose the original declaration of the custodian with the records. Seal the envelope. (2) Attach a copy of this subpoena to the envelope or write on the envelope the case name and number; your name; and the date, time, and place from item 1 in the box above. (3) Place this first envelope in an outer envelope, seal it, and mail it to the clerk of the court at the address in item 1. (4) Mail a copy of your declaration to the attorney or party listed at the top of this form.

4. IF YOU HAVE ANY QUESTIONS ABOUT THE TIME OR DATE YOU ARE TO APPEAR, OR IF YOU WANT TO BE CERTAIN THAT YOUR PRESENCE IS REQUIRED, CONTACT THE FOLLOWING PERSON BEFORE THE DATE ON WHICH YOU ARE TO APPEAR:
   a. Name of subpoenaing party or attorney: b. Telephone number:

5. **Witness Fees:** You are entitled to witness fees and mileage actually traveled both ways, as provided by law, if you request them at the time of service. You may request them before your scheduled appearance from the person named in item 4.

> DISOBEDIENCE OF THIS SUBPOENA MAY BE PUNISHED AS CONTEMPT BY THIS COURT. YOU WILL ALSO BE LIABLE FOR THE SUM OF FIVE HUNDRED DOLLARS AND ALL DAMAGES RESULTING FROM YOUR FAILURE TO OBEY.

Date issued:

▶ _____

_____   (SIGNATURE OF PERSON ISSUING SUBPOENA)
(TYPE OR PRINT NAME)

(Declaration in support of subpoena on reverse)   (TITLE)

Form Adopted for Mandatory Use Judicial Council of California SUBP-002 [Rev. January 1, 2007]	CIVIL SUBPOENA (DUCES TECUM) FOR PERSONAL APPEARANCE AND PRODUCTION OF DOCUMENTS AND THINGS AT TRIAL OR HEARING AND DECLARATION	Page 1 of 3 Code of Civil Procedure, § 1985 et seq.

American LegalNet, Inc.
www.Forms*Workflow*.com

SUBP-002

PLAINTIFF/PETITIONER: Robin Plaintiff	CASE NUMBER:
DEFENDANT/RESPONDENT: Joe Defendant	741827

The production of the documents or the other things sought by the subpoena on page one is supported by *(check one)*:
☐ the attached affidavit or declaration ☒ the following declaration:

DECLARATION IN SUPPORT OF CIVIL SUBPOENA (DUCES TECUM) FOR PERSONAL APPEARANCE AND PRODUCTION OF DOCUMENTS AND THINGS AT TRIAL OR HEARING
(Code Civ. Proc., §§ 1985, 1987.5)

1. I, the undersigned, declare I am the ☒ plaintiff ☐ defendant ☐ petitioner ☐ respondent
☐ attorney for *(specify)*: ☐ other *(specify)*:
in the above-entitled action.

2. The witness has possession or control of the following documents or other things and shall produce them at the time and place specified in the *Civil Subpoena for Personal Appearance and Production of Documents and Things at Trial or Hearing* on page one of this form *(specify the exact documents or other things to be produced)*:

Savings account records

☐ Continued on Attachment 2.

3. Good cause exists for the production of the documents or other things described in paragraph 2 for the following reasons:

Judgment remains unsatisfied and defendant has failed to voluntarily reveal his assets.

☐ Continued on Attachment 3.

4. These documents or other things described in paragraph 2 are material to the issues involved in this case for the following reasons:

These documents will reveal defendants assets.

☐ Continued on Attachment 4.

I declare under penalty of perjury under the laws of the State of California that the foregoing is true and correct.

Date: 1/10/07

............Robin..Plaintiff................................ ▶ *Robin Plaintiff*
(TYPE OR PRINT NAME) (SIGNATURE OF ☐ SUBPOENAING PARTY ☐ ATTORNEY FOR SUBPOENAING PARTY)

(Proof of service on page three) Page 2 of 3

SUBP-002 [Rev. January 1, 2007] **CIVIL SUBPOENA (DUCES TECUM) FOR PERSONAL APPEARANCE AND PRODUCTION OF DOCUMENTS AND THINGS AT TRIAL OR HEARING AND DECLARATION**

SUBP-002

	CASE NUMBER:
PLAINTIFF/PETITIONER: Robin Plaintiff	741827
DEFENDANT/RESPONDENT: Joe Defendant	

PROOF OF SERVICE OF CIVIL SUBPOENA (DUCES TECUM)
FOR PERSONAL APPEARANCE AND PRODUCTION OF DOCUMENTS
AND THINGS AT TRIAL OR HEARING AND DECLARATION

1. I served this *Civil Subpoena (Duces Tecum) for Personal Appearance and Production of Documents and Things at Trial or Hearing and Declaration* by personally delivering a copy to the person served as follows:

 a. Person served *(name)*: Joe Defendant

 b. Address where served: 228 Jackson Avenue
 Big City, CA 94443

 c. Date of delivery: 1/11/07

 d. Time of delivery: 9:00 A.M.

 e. Witness fees *(check one)*:
 (1) ☐ were offered or demanded
 and paid. Amount: ...... $ _____
 (2) ☒ were not demanded or paid.

 f. Fee for service: .... $ _____

2. I received this subpoena for service on *(date)*:

3. Person serving:
 a. ☒ Not a registered California process server.
 b. ☐ California sheriff or marshal.
 c. ☐ Registered California process server.
 d. ☐ Employee or independent contractor of a registered California process server.
 e. ☐ Exempt from registration under Business and Professions Code section 22350(b).
 f. ☐ Registered professional photocopier.
 g. ☐ Exempt from registration under Business and Professions Code section 22451.
 h. Name, address, telephone number, and, if applicable, county of registration and number:

I **declare** under penalty of perjury under the laws of the State of California that the foregoing is true and correct.	**(For California sheriff or marshal use only)** I **certify** that the foregoing is true and correct.
Date: 1/11/07	Date:
▶ _____Bobby Neighbor_____ (SIGNATURE)	▶ *Bobby Neighbor* (SIGNATURE)

Page 3 of 3

SUBP-002 [Rev. January 1, 2007]   **PROOF OF SERVICE OF CIVIL SUBPOENA (DUCES TECUM) FOR PERSONAL APPEARANCE AND PRODUCTION OF DOCUMENTS AND THINGS AT TRIAL OR HEARING AND DECLARATION**

EJ-100

ATTORNEY OR PARTY WITHOUT ATTORNEY *(Name, State Bar number, and address)*:
After recording return to:

Robin Plaintiff
123 Smith Street
Big City, CA 94444

TELEPHONE NO.:

FAX NO. *(Optional)*:

E-MAIL ADDRESS *(Optional)*:

ATTORNEY FOR *(Name)*:

SUPERIOR COURT OF CALIFORNIA, COUNTY OF

STREET ADDRESS: Superior Court of Big City

MAILING ADDRESS: 222 Justice Way

CITY AND ZIP CODE: Big City, CA 94444

BRANCH NAME:

FOR RECORDER'S OR SECRETARY OF STATE'S USE ONLY

PLAINTIFF: Robin Plaintiff

DEFENDANT: Joe Defendant

CASE NUMBER:

741827

ACKNOWLEDGMENT OF SATISFACTION OF JUDGMENT

☒ FULL ☐ PARTIAL ☐ MATURED INSTALLMENT

FOR COURT USE ONLY

1. Satisfaction of the judgment is acknowledged as follows:
   a. ☒ Full satisfaction
      (1) ☒ Judgment is satisfied in full.
      (2) ☐ The judgment creditor has accepted payment or performance other than that specified in the judgment in full satisfaction of the judgment.
   b. ☐ Partial satisfaction
      The amount received in partial satisfaction of the judgment is $
   c. ☐ Matured installment
      All matured installments under the installment judgment have been satisfied as of *(date)*:

2. Full name and address of judgment creditor:* Robin Plaintiff
   123 Smith Street
   Big City, CA 94444

3. Full name and address of assignee of record, if any:

   N/A

4. Full name and address of judgment debtor being fully or partially released:* Joe Defendant
   228 Jackson Avenue
   Big City, CA 94443

5. a. Judgment entered on *(date)*: 1/1/98
   b. ☒ Renewal entered on *(date)*: 1/2/07

6. ☒ An ☒ abstract of judgment ☐ certified copy of the judgment has been recorded as follows *(complete all information for each county where recorded)*:

COUNTY	DATE OF RECORDING	INSTRUMENT NUMBER
Big City, CA	1/12/07	421723814

7. ☐ A notice of judgment lien has been filed in the office of the Secretary of State as file number *(specify)*:

NOTICE TO JUDGMENT DEBTOR: If this is an acknowledgment of full satisfaction of judgment, it will have to be recorded in each county shown in item 6 above, if any, in order to release the judgment lien, and will have to be filed in the office of the Secretary of State to terminate any judgment lien on personal property.

Date: 3/1/07

▶ *Robin Plaintiff*

*(SIGNATURE OF JUDGMENT CREDITOR OR ASSIGNEE OF CREDITOR OR ATTORNEY**)*

Page 1 of 1

*The names of the judgment creditor and judgment debtor must be stated as shown in any Abstract of Judgment which was recorded and is being released by this satisfaction. ** A separate notary acknowledgment must be attached for each signature.

Form Approved for Optional Use
Judicial Council of California
EJ-100 [Rev. January 1, 2005]

ACKNOWLEDGMENT OF SATISFACTION OF JUDGMENT

Code of Civil Procedure, §§ 724.060,
724.120, 724.250

American LegalNet, Inc.
www.USCourtForms.com

ATTORNEY OR PARTY WITHOUT ATTORNEY *(Name and Address)*:

☐ Recording requested by and return to:

Robin Plaintiff
123 Smith Street
Big City, CA 94444

TELEPHONE NO.:

FOR RECORDER'S USE ONLY

ATTORNEY FOR *(Name)*:

NAME OF COURT: Superior Court of Big City
STREET ADDRESS: 222 Justice Way
MAILING ADDRESS: Big City, CA 94444
CITY AND ZIP CODE:
BRANCH NAME:

PLAINTIFF: Robin Plaintiff

DEFENDANT: Joe Defendant

MEMORANDUM OF GARNISHEE
(Attachment —Enforcement of Judgment)

LEVYING OFFICER *(Name and Address)*:

Sam Sheriff
111 Justice Way
Big City, CA 94444

NOTICE TO PERSON SERVED WITH WRIT AND NOTICE OF LEVY OR NOTICE OF ATTACHMENT: This memorandum must be completed and mailed or delivered to the levying officer within 10 days after service on you of the writ and notice of levy or attachment unless you have fully complied with the levy. Failure to complete and return this memorandum may render you liable for the costs and attorney fees incurred in obtaining the required information.
– RETURN ALL COPIES OF THIS MEMORANDUM TO THE LEVYING OFFICER –

LEVYING OFFICER FILE NO.	COURT CASE NO.
0754321	741827

This memorandum does *not* apply to garnishment of earnings.

1. If you will not deliver to the levying officer any property levied upon, describe the property and the reason for not delivering it:

Not applicable

2. **For writ of execution only**   Describe any property of the judgment debtor not levied upon that is in your possession or under your control:

laptop computer
flat screen television
$400.00 cash

3. If you owe money to the judgment debtor which you will not pay to the levying officer, describe the amount and terms of the obligation and the reason for not paying it to the levying officer:

I don't owe Joe Defendant any money. I'm holding his $400.00 for him.

(Continued on reverse)

Form Approved by the
Judicial Council of California
AT-167, EJ-152 [New July 1, 1983]

MEMORANDUM OF GARNISHEE
(Attachment — Enforcement of Judgment)

CCP 488.610
701.030

American LegalNet, Inc.
www.USCourtForms.com

SHORT TITLE:	LEVYING OFFICER FILE NO.:	COURT CASE NO.:
Robin Plaintiff v. Joe Defendant	0754321	741827

4. Describe the amount and terms of any obligation owed to the judgment debtor that is levied upon but is not yet due and payable:

NOT APPLICABLE

5. **For writ of execution only**   Describe the amount and terms of any obligation owed to the judgment debtor that is not levied upon:

NOT APPLICABLE

6. Describe any claims and rights of other persons to the property or obligation levied upon that are known to you and the names and addresses of the other persons:

NOT APPLICABLE

DECLARATION

I declare under penalty of perjury under the laws of the State of California that the foregoing is true and correct.

Date: 3.1.07

................Karen Cousin...............   ▶ *Karen Cousin*
(TYPE OR PRINT NAME)   (SIGNATURE)

If you need more space to provide the information required by this memorandum, you may attach additional pages.

☐ Total number of pages attached:

AT-167, EJ-152 [New July 1, 1983]

MEMORANDUM OF GARNISHEE
(Attachment — Enforcement of Judgment)

Page two

WG-010/EJ-175

ATTORNEY OR PARTY WITHOUT ATTORNEY *(Name, State Bar number, and address)*:	TELEPHONE NO.:	FOR COURT USE ONLY

Robin Plaintiff
123 Smith Street
Big City, CA 94444

ATTORNEY FOR *(Name)*:

NAME OF COURT, JUDICIAL DISTRICT OR BRANCH COURT, IF ANY: Superior Court of Big City
222 Justice Way
Big City, CA 94444

PLAINTIFF: Robin Plaintiff

DEFENDANT: Joe Defendant

LEVYING OFFICER FILE NO.: 0754321

NOTICE OF HEARING ON CLAIM OF EXEMPTION (Wage Garnishment—Enforcement of Judgment)	COURT CASE NO.: 741827

1. TO:

   Name and address of levying officer

   Sam Sheriff
   111 Justice Way
   Big City, CA 94444

   Name and address of judgment debtor

   Joe Defendant
   228 Jackson Avenue
   Big City, CA 94444

   ☐ Claimant, if other than judgment debtor
   (name and address):

   ☐ Judgment debtor's attorney
   (name and address):

2. **A hearing to determine the claim of exemption of**
   ☒ judgment debtor
   ☐ other claimant
   will be held as follows:

   a. date: 2.28.07   time: 9:30 A.M. ☒ dept.: 238   ☐ div.:   ☒ rm.: 238

   b. address of court:

3. ☐ The judgment creditor will not appear at the hearing and submits the issue on the papers filed with the court.

Date: 2.15.07

Robin Plaintiff
....
(TYPE OR PRINT NAME)

▶ *Robin Plaintiff*
(SIGNATURE OF JUDGMENT CREDITOR OR ATTORNEY)

If you do not attend the hearing, the court may determine your claim based on the Claim of Exemption, Financial Statement (when one is required), Notice of Opposition to Claim of Exemption, and other evidence that may be presented.

Page 1 of 2

NOTICE OF HEARING ON CLAIM OF EXEMPTION
(Wage Garnishment—Enforcement of Judgment)

Code of Civil Procedure, § 703.550, 706.107
www.courtinfo.ca.gov

		WG-010/EJ-175
SHORT TITLE:	LEVYING OFFICER FILE NO.	0754321
Robin Plaintiff v. Joe Defendant	COURT CASE NO.	741827

PROOF OF SERVICE BY MAIL

I am over the age of 18 and not a party to this cause. I am a resident of or employed in the county where the mailing occurred. My residence or business address is *(specify)*:

I served the attached Notice of Hearing on Claim of Exemption and the attached Notice of Opposition to Claim of Exemption by enclosing true copies in a sealed envelope addressed to each person whose name and address is given below and depositing the envelope in the United States mail with the postage fully prepaid.

(1)   Date of deposit: 2.16.07   (2)   Place of deposit *(city and state)*: Big City, CA

NAME AND ADDRESS OF EACH PERSON TO WHOM NOTICE WAS MAILED

Joe Defendant
228 Jackson Avenue
Big City, CA 94444

I declare under penalty of perjury under the laws of the State of California that the foregoing is true and correct.

Date: 2.16.07

Frank Friend	▶ *Frank Friend*
(TYPE OR PRINT NAME)	*(SIGNATURE OF DECLARANT)*

PROOF OF SERVICE—PERSONAL DELIVERY

I am over the age of 18 and not a party to this cause. My residence or business address is *(specify)*:

I served the attached Notice of Hearing on Claim of Exemption and the attached Notice of Opposition to Claim of Exemption by personally delivering copies to the person served as shown below.

PERSONS SERVED

Name	**Delivery At**		
	Date:	Time:	Address:

I declare under penalty of perjury under the laws of the State of California that the foregoing is true and correct.

Date:

	▶	
(TYPE OR PRINT NAME)		*(SIGNATURE OF DECLARANT)*

WG-010/WJ-175 [Rev. January 1, 2007]	**NOTICE OF HEARING ON CLAIM OF EXEMPTION** (Wage Garnishment—Enforcement of Judgment)	Page 2 of 2

1 Name: Robin Plaintiff
2 Address: 123 Smith Street
          Big City, CA 94444
3 Telephone:
4
5
6
7   ____SUPERIOR____   **COURT OF** __BIG CITY__
8   **COUNTY OF** _____
9
10   Robin Plaintiff   Case No.: 741827
11   Plaintiff,   NOTICE OF MOTION AND MOTION
                                     FOR ASSIGNMENT OF ORDER RIGHT TO
12   PAYMENT; MEMORANDUM OF POINTS
                                     AND AUTHORITIES; DECLARATION
13   Vs.   IN SUPPORT OF MOTION; ORDER
14   Joe Defendant
15   Defendant,
16
17   _____
18   TO: __Joe Defendant_____
19   NOTICE IS HEREBY GIVEN that **Robin Plaintiff**_____
20   Will, on **March 8, 2007**_____, at **9:00 A.M.**,
21   in Department **284** of the above-entitled court located at
22   **222 Justice Way**_____ (Address), **Big City**____ (City),
23   ____**CA**_____ (State), move for an order that the
24   judgment debtor in this action assign to **Robin Plaintiff**_____,
25   judgment creditor, all or part of a right to payment due or to
26   become due to **Joe Defendant**_____, judgment debtor.
27   This motion will be based on this Notice of Motion, Memorandum of
28   Points and Authorities, on the Declaration of **Robin Plaintiff**_____

                    Motion for Order Assigning Right to Payment - 1

1 served and Filed herewith, the papers and records on file herein, and

2 on such oral and documentary evidence as may be presented at the

3 Hearing of this motion.

4

5 Dated: **2.8.07**

6

7 Name: *Robin Plaintiff*

8

9 ### MEMORANDUM OF POINTS AND AUTHORITIES

10   Where the judgment debtor is entitled to receive payments,

11 Either presently or in the future, the Court may order the

12 judgment debtor to assign to the judgment creditor or a receiver

13 appointed by the Court all or a part of such payment.

14 (C.C.P. § 708.510)

15

16

17 ### DECLARATION

18   I, the undersigned, declare as follows:

19   1.   I am the judgment creditor in the above-entitled

20 Action.

21   2.   On ___1/1/98___, I received judgment against

22 ___Joe Defendant___, as follows: $ __9440.00__ .

23

24   3.   The amount $ __1850.00__ remains unsatisfied

25 (this sum includes the unpaid portion of the original judgment,

26 interest and costs per Memorandum of Costs After Judgment filed

27 on __1/2/07__ .)

28

Motion for Order Assigning Right to Payment - 2

1   4. I am informed, believe, and allege on such

2   Information and belief, that the judgment debtor in this action

3   Is either:

4   ✕   entitled to recover future payments from

5   _____ Nick Neighbor—$200.00 due immediately _____; or

6   ( )   an employee of the federal government,

7   presently working at _____.

8   Pursuant to (INSERT CODE SECTION THAT SUPPORTS YOUR RIGHT TO RECEIVE

9   PAYMENTS)

10   5. I request an order that judgment debtor assign to me as the

11 Judgment creditor, all payments to be received from the

12 Aforementioned source until the judgment is satisfied or until

13 Further order of the court.

14   I declare under penalty of perjury that the foregoing is

15 True and correct and if called as a witness I could competently

16 Testify thereto.

17   Executed in   **Big City, California.**

18

19 Dated: ___ **2/8/07** _____   Name: *Robin Plaintiff*

20

21

22

23

24

25

26

27

28

Appendix D:
Blank Forms

This appendix contains blank versions of letters and a debtor examination questionnaire that you may want to use in your own judgment collection. Be sure to make the copies on 8.5"x11" paper if you make photocopies of these forms.

DEMAND LETTER

Debtor's Name
Debtor's Address
City, State Zip

Dear Debtor,

The judgment entered by the _____ (enter name of court) on _____, 20___ (enter date) against you in the amount of _____ (enter amount) is now due. You are no longer permitted to appeal the court's decision. Therefore, I am asking that you pay your judgment immediately.

If payment is not received by _____, 20___ (enter date one/two weeks from date of mailing) at 5:00 p.m., I will be forced to initiate collection procedures against you. To prevent further damage to your credit report and additional expenses added to your judgment, please forward payment to the following address immediately.

_____

_____

_____

Sincerely,

This page intentionally left blank.

LETTER TO EMPLOYER TO FOLLOW WAGE GARNISHMENT

_____(employer's name)

_____

_____

Dear _____ (employer's name),

It has been _____ since you were served with a wage garnishment/earnings withholding order from the_____ Sheriff's Department, file #_____. You may not be aware, but _____ Code Section _____ requires that you honor this order if _____ is currently employed by your company. You were served the Employer's Return form and have not returned it to the _____ County Sheriff's Department as of today.

We are writing to encourage you to abide by the above-referenced law and obey the withholding order immediately or submit the Employer's Return form. If you fail to obey the order, you may become liable for the underlying debt of your employee.

If you have questions concerning your legal rights and responsibilities concerning this court order, contact your private attorney immediately. We do not want to have to take any legal action to implement this order, but are prepared to do so if necessary.

Sincerely,

This page intentionally left blank.

INDIVIDUAL DEBTOR EXAMINATION QUESTIONNAIRE

PERSONAL INFORMATION

Full legal name _____ Age _____

Sex _____

Social Security number _____

Driver's license number _____ State _____

Height _____ Weight _____ Hair color _____

Eye Color _____ Race _____

Current address

_____

Current phone number (Home) _____

(Work) _____

If at current address for less than 5 years, please provide last address:

_____

Have you ever been married? _____ If yes, when and to whom:

_____

_____

Do you have any children? _____ If yes, please provide name and age:

_____

INSURANCE

Do you have a life insurance policy on yourself? _____ If yes, with whom and how much is the policy's value?

_____

_____

What is the policy number? _____

Have you ever taken a loan against the policy? _____

If yes, when and how much? _____

REAL PROPERTY (REAL ESTATE)

Do you own your home? _____ If yes, what is the address?

_____

_____

_____

HOME OWNERS (If you are not a home owner, skip this section)
If you own your home, what is its current value?

_____

If you own your home, how much is your monthly mortgage payment?

_____

RENTERS
If you do not own your home, who does? _____
Please provide name, address, and phone number:

_____

_____

_____

If you do not own your home, how much monthly rent do you pay?

_____

If you do not own your home, do you pay your rent by cash or check?

_____

PERSONAL PROPERTY
Do you own a car? _____ If yes, provide year, make, and model:

_____

_____

Do you owe money on your car? _____ If yes, to whom?

_____

_____

BANK ACCOUNTS
Do you have a checking account? _____ If yes, please give bank, branch, and account number:

_____

_____

Do you have a savings account? _____ If yes, please give bank, branch, and account number:

_____

_____

STOCK

Do you own any stocks? _____ If yes, please list the name of the stock, how many shares, and the brokerage firm through which you bought these stocks:

_____

_____

_____

_____

SAFE-DEPOSIT BOX

Do you have a safe-deposit box? _____ If yes, which bank is it in?

_____

What is in your safe-deposit box?

_____

_____

_____

_____

DEBTS OWED TO DEBTOR

Does anyone owe you any money? _____ If yes, please name and provide the details of the debt:

_____

_____

_____

_____

_____

OTHER LAWSUITS

Are you a plaintiff in any lawsuits? _____
If yes, please provide the following:
Case number: _____ County in which case is filed: _____
Defendant's name:

_____

Type of case:

_____

Prayer amount:

_____

Does anyone owe you any money? _____ If yes, please name and
provide the details of the debt:

_____

_____

_____

_____

Are you a plaintiff in any lawsuits? _____ If yes, please provide the
following:
Case number: _____ County in which case is filed? _____
Defendant's name:

_____

Type of case:

_____

Prayer amount:

_____

Does anyone owe you any money? _____ If yes, please name and
provide the details of the debt:

_____

_____

_____

OTHER SOURCES OF INCOME

Do you receive income from any other source than your full-time employer? If yes, please describe:

1.

_____

_____

_____

2.

_____

_____

_____

3.

_____

_____

_____

4.

_____

_____

_____

5.

_____

_____

_____

EMPLOYMENT

What is your occupation?

_____

Do you hold any professional licenses, in this state or any other? _____
If yes, please list and describe:

_____

_____

_____

Current employer:

_____

Employer's address:

_____

_____

Employer's phone number:

_____

Fax number:

_____

Job title:

_____

Supervisor's name:

_____

Last employer:

_____

Employer's address:

_____

_____

Employer's phone number:

_____

Fax number:

_____

Job title:

_____

Supervisor's name:

_____

EXPENSES
Monthly Household Expenses
a. Rent or mortgage payment:

_____

b. Food:

_____

c. Clothing:

_____

d. Medical and dental payments:

_____

e. Child support:

_____

f. Spousal support:

_____

g. Laundry/cleaning supplies:

_____

h. Transportation:

_____

i. Monthly installment payments:

_____

j. Other expenses:

_____

_____

_____

_____

_____

AT THE HEARING

Do you have any jewelry on your person that individually is worth more than $10.00?

_____ If yes, please show it to me and describe it.

Do you have any cash or change on your person right now?

_____ If yes, how much?

Please provide a detailed description of any asset(s) that has not been addressed above:

_____

_____

_____

_____

_____

_____

_____

_____

_____

_____

_____

_____

_____

BUSINESS DEBTOR EXAMINATION QUESTIONNAIRE

Name of business:

_____

Address:

_____

Phone number: _____ Fax: _____
E-mail: _____
Type of business:

_____

Organization: (Please circle one)
- Sole Proprietorship
- Partnership
- Limited Liability Company (LLC)
- Limited Partnership (LP)
- Corporation

BANK ACCOUNTS
Do you have a checking account? _____ If yes, please give bank, branch, and account number:

_____

Do you have a savings account? _____ If yes, please give bank, branch, and account number:

_____

_____

STOCK

Do you own any stocks? _____ If yes, please list the name of the stock, how many shares, and the brokerage firm through which you bought these stocks:

_____

_____

_____

_____

_____

_____

_____

SAFE-DEPOSIT BOX

Do you have a safe-deposit box? _____ If yes, which bank is it in? _____What is in your safe-deposit box?

_____

_____

_____

_____

Are you a plaintiff in any lawsuits? _____
If yes, please provide the following:
Case number: _____ County in which case is filed: _____

Defendant's name:

_____

Type of case:

_____

Prayer amount:

_____

Case number: _____ County in which case is filed: _____

Defendant's name:

_____

Type of case:

_____

Prayer amount:

_____

Case number: _____ County in which case is filed: _____

Defendant's name:

_____

Type of case:

_____

Prayer amount:

_____

ACCOUNTS RECEIVABLE

Please list all of your accounts receivable and the current amount due.

Name: _____

Account #: _____

Amount due: _____

Address:

_____

Phone number: _____ Fax number: _____

Contact person: _____

Name: _____ Account #: _____

Amount due: _____

Address:

_____

Phone number: _____ Fax number: _____

Contact person: _____

Name: _____ Account #: _____

Name: _____ Account #: _____

Amount due: _____

Address:

_____

Phone number: _____ Fax number: _____
Contact person: _____
Name: _____ Account #: _____
Amount due: _____
Address:

_____

Phone number: _____ Fax number: _____
Contact person: _____
Name: _____ Account #: _____
Amount due: _____
Address:

_____

Phone number: _____ Fax number: _____
Contact person: _____

OFFICE EQUIPMENT

Please list the office furniture that you own:

Describe piece:

_____

Brand name:

_____

Fair market value:

_____

Condition:

_____

Describe piece:

_____

Brand name:

_____

Fair market value:

_____

Condition:

_____

Describe piece:

_____

Brand name:

_____

Fair market value:

_____

Condition:

_____

Describe piece:

_____

Brand name:

_____

Fair market value:

_____

Condition:

_____

Describe piece:

_____

Brand name:

_____

Fair market value:

_____

Condition:

_____

Describe piece:

_____

Brand name:

_____

Fair market value:

_____

Condition:

_____

Describe piece:

_____

Brand name:

_____

Fair market value:

_____

Condition:

_____

REAL PROPERTY

Do you own the property in which your business is located? _____

If yes, do you have a mortgage on it? _____

If yes, please provide the bank's name, address, phone:

_____

_____

_____

Do you own any other real property?

_____

If yes, please provide the following information:

Address:

_____

_____

Description:

_____

_____

Mortgage amount:

_____

Bank:

_____

Existing liens:

_____

If yes, please describe:

_____

Co-owners:

_____

Address of co-owner:

_____

Phone:

_____

Address:

_____

Description:

_____

Mortgage amount:

_____

Bank:

_____

Existing liens:

_____

If yes, please describe:

_____

Co-owners:

_____

Address of Co-owner:

_____

Phone:

_____

Address:

_____

Description:

_____

Mortgage amount:

_____

Bank:

_____

Existing liens:

_____

If yes, please describe:

_____

Co-owners:

_____

Address of co-owner:

_____

Phone:

_____

Address:

_____

Description:

_____

Mortgage amount:

_____

Bank:

_____

Existing liens:

_____

If yes, please describe:

_____

Co-owners:

_____

Address of co-owner:

_____

Phone:

_____

Please provide a detailed description of any asset(s) that has not been addressed above:

_____

_____

_____

_____

_____

_____

_____

_____

_____

_____

_____

_____

_____

Index

About the Author

Adrienne M. McMillan is a staff attorney with the San Francisco superior court's self-help center, The ACCESS Center. She earned her bachelor's degree from George Mason University. She holds a Master's in English from San Francisco State University and a JD from Golden Gate University School of Law.